ACCELERATING YOUR AGENCY

AN 8 SYSTEM PLAYBOOK FOR GROWING YOUR AGENCY FASTER

Jason Swenk

Accelerating Your Agency:

An 8 System Playbook For Growing Your Agency Faster

Published by Swenk It Books

Atlanta, GA

Copyright © 2018 by Jason Swenk.

All rights reserved. Printed in the United States of America. Except as permitted under the United States Copyright Act of 1976, no part of this publication may be reproduced, scanned, or distributed in any print or electronic form or by any means, or stored in a database or retrieval system, without permission of the publisher. Please do not participate in or encourage piracy of copyrighted materials in violation of the author's rights. Purchase only authorized editions.

ISBN: 978-1717596215

Printed in the United States of America

TABLE OF CONTENTS

INTRODUCTION..1

SYSTEM 1: CLARITY..7
Lesson 1.1: Defining A Clear Path..9
Lesson 1.2: Creating a 90-Day Action Plan.........................19
System 1 Recap..25

System 2: POSITIONING...27
Lesson 2.1: Identifying Your Niche & Specialization..........29
Lesson 2.2: Positioning as "The Choice" Rather Than "A Choice".....33
Lesson 2.3: Crafting an Elevator Pitch................................38
Lesson 2.4: Agency Website Makeover...............................42
System 2 Recap..50

System 3: OFFERING..53
Lesson 3.1: Creating a Service Offering Ladder..................54
Lesson 3.2: Pricing to Achieve Financial Goals...................59
Lesson 3.3: Determining the Best Pricing Model................62
System 3 Recap..69

System 4: PROSPECTING..73
Lesson 4.1: Low-Hanging Fruit...74
Lesson 4.2: Outbound Strategies..77
Lesson 4.3: Inbound Strategies...80
Lesson 4.4: Strategic Partnerships......................................89
Lesson 4.5: Building a Community....................................90
Lesson 4.6: The ABC's of Marketing Automation..............92
System 4 Recap..97

System 5: SALES..........101
Lesson 5.1: Qualifying Prospects..........102
Lesson 5.2: Managing Sales Stages..........106
Lesson 5.3: Creating Proposals that Win..........108
Lesson 5.4: Increasing Your Chances for Yes..........117
Lesson 5.5: Following-Up After A Pitch..........124
Lesson 5.6: Building a Sales Team..........126
System 5 Recap..........131

System 6: DELIVERY..........135
Lesson 6.1: Streamlining Delivery..........136
Lesson 6.2: Eliminating Profit Leaks..........139
System 6 Recap..........144

System 7: OPERATIONS..........147
Lesson 7.1: Building a Team..........148
Lesson 7.2: Improving Cash Flow..........153
System 7 Recap..........161

System 8: LEADERSHIP..........163
Lesson 8.1: Becoming the CEO..........164
Lesson 8.2: Incentivizing Employees..........170
Lesson 8.3: Determining Valuation..........176
Lesson 8.4: Being Acquired..........181
Lesson 8.5: Putting It All Together..........185
System 8 Recap..........187

CONCLUSION..........191

DEDICATION..........192

CITATION OF RESOURCES..........194

INTRODUCTION

"Winning is not a sometime thing; it's an all the time thing. You don't win once in awhile; you don't do things right once in awhile; you do them right all of the time. Winning is a habit. Unfortunately, so is losing."
~ Vince Lombardi

Let's be clear. This book isn't a silver bullet to a bigger, better agency. There's no such thing. What this book is, though, is the eight systems you'll need for accelerating your agency's growth. It will change your entire approach to leading an agency but the hard work and hustle is still yours. Learn it, implement it and then win at it. Win hard and make winning your habit.

To date, we have helped over 20,000 agency owners in 42 countries build a more profitable, successful and enjoyable agency business. Some have said having these eight systems from inception would have shaved up to five years off their initial learning curve. (Hindsight is always 20/20 though.) I say, don't look back. Keep your eyes on road and enjoy the ride.

As you move ahead in this book, I encourage you to do these two things:

1. **Read each system in order.** The eight systems are designed to roll up into one another. They're explained in a specific order and each system builds upon the ones prior. Jumping ahead won't help you grow any faster, and might even have the opposite effect.

2. **Take action right away.** This isn't the kind of book you read from cover to cover. You will need to implement some things in one system before you move onto the next system, and so on. You might want to think of this more like a textbook where each lesson builds on the one prior.

You see, I owned my digital agency for twelve years before selling it. Like that of so many other entrepreneurs, one of my daily habits was checking email right away. This is actually a terrible habit of allowing the messages in my inbox dictate the direction my day was headed. It's not a great habit, but it was mine back then nonetheless.

One morning I woke up and was checking my email before heading into the office. I remember very clearly reading the email that changed everything. There was a problem and one of my employees had emailed me about it; we were on the verge of losing our biggest client. The client was planning to leave in order to work with another agency. I took a brief moment to think about it but couldn't wrap my head around what happened. We had a great relationship (I thought) and always delivered above and beyond expectation (I thought). So why was this happening out of the blue?

I got to the office that morning and talked with the team, trying to pinpoint reasons or issues that would make a client leave us. The team had no clue either. After a couple days of being pissed off and worried about what we were going to do, I started to figure it out...

The problem wasn't anything we did or didn't DO. The problem was what we didn't say, didn't share, and didn't reveal. I never really put any energy behind communicating the agency's mission, vision, or direction. There was no real clarity on where the agency was headed, I never dedicated any time or effort toward it and never articulated it to my team.

I had started the agency spontaneously when someone asked me to design a website that they would pay me to create. Like many other entrepreneurs, it was a business that came about simply because I knew how to do something cool that other people wanted and were willing to pay for. After that first one it was another website, and another, until side jobs became regular work and it grew bigger than me. I didn't have any real direction on where I wanted to go - I was just along for the ride.

However, in crisis mode I was forced to spend some time reflecting, and that's when I realized, this big client didn't just want to be "along for the ride." They wanted to know where they were going. They had choices and needed a clear reason why they should continue choosing us.

What I realized was that I needed to step back and gain some clarity. I needed to identify the vision for my agency that could be communicated internally as well as externally. No more assumptions that anyone wants to be "along for the ride." We needed to define who we were and what we stood for - because it's so much easier to get where you're going when you have a destination in mind. Doing this meant defining our perfect clients, identifying which services were most profitable, and deciding where we wanted to take the agency and why.

Without clarity, we were taking on the wrong client, saying yes to the wrong engagements, and causing employees uncertainty. It had all just snowballed. Sure, I was committed to winning but I wasn't exhibiting the skills we needed for winning. With this revelation, I dedicated myself to making a habit of winning. We started the process of creating and documenting systems for the business. It was a long, hard road, but ultimately worth the journey.

Winning Is A Habit.

As Vince Lombardi put it, "Winning is a habit. Unfortunately, so is losing." As with any habit, positive or negative, it takes time to develop. It's something that goes from being occasional or accidental to being routine or systematic. For example, a lot of people don't make their bed in the morning. What would it take to make that a habit? The answer: **commitment and a plan.** That non-bed maker just needs to commit to making his bed and then plan out when and how to make it happen. The plan would just need to be something like: wake up, take a shower, get dressed, make the bed, then continue with the morning routine of breakfast and head to work. By creating a system, the task gets done with very little issue. Bed made = WIN!

The same is true for developing a winning agency business. It just takes **commitment and a plan.** Developing a winning habit for your agency is as simple as committing to it and following a plan. It takes time, but **having all the right systems** in place for success is the only way. I know agency ownership can be lonely and very isolating. Sometimes you wind up questioning your ability to juggle it all. You sometimes feel like you've got to fake it until you make it. You may find yourself second guessing your decisions and yet, you've got no one to bounce things off of.

I know - I've been there!

That's why I've developed resources like this as well as online communities for agency owners. This book is packed with my 17+ years experience, plus all the information, tactics, processes, and tools I used to build a multi-million dollar agency that I started, enjoyed, scaled, and sold. Join the conversation online for free at: https://jasonswenk.com/community

There are 8 Systems for a reason.

I believe that systems outperform talent. Having the right systems in place is the difference between a struggling entrepreneur and a successful one. So, I drilled down to the core of what makes a sustainable and thriving marketing agency.

I know you're excited and you may have a specific issue (like Prospecting, which is System 4). I urge you not to jump ahead! I know you're anxious, energized, and ready to take action. Stick with me on this; I promise it'll be worth it :)

Whether your business is in its infancy or more mature, but somewhat stagnant state, there is relevancy among these pages based on the execution of my method - **but you have to go in order.**

INTRODUCTION

With that said, you can work at your own pace. Read a lesson, do the "homework" and execute. This can take you eight days, eight weeks or eight months. Work at your own pace; give each System 100%, but go in order. Seriously. There's no sense in jumping to System 4: Prospecting, if you haven't gone through Systems 1-3, which define your vision, your positioning, and your offering.

This framework will work if you work through it sequentially. So, now that you know what you're in for - let's do this!

SYSTEM 1

1
Clarity

If you've lost sight of why you do what you do, you're missing clarity. Are you the tollbooth owner? Does your team need to pass everything through you before they can move forward? Whether that's intentional micromanaging or not, it's not healthy or scalable. If your team comes to you too often for direction or is afraid to make decisions without you, it's probably because they do not understand your company vision and goals.

In this chapter, you'll learn:

1. How to determine and write your company vision.
2. The importance of sharing and communicating the vision with your team.
3. How to define your role, including what you need to be doing and what you shouldn't be doing.

This first System is all about identifying your vision and creating a crystal clear path to get where you want to go. This is probably the most important and yet, most overlooked element to building a successful agency.

I think most of us just sort of just fall into the agency business. I've interviewed over a hundred agency owners and all the stories have a familiar tune. Most start as a freelancer, or doing side jobs in addition to their regular, full time gig. Before they know it, the side jobs or freelance projects become more frequent, more fun, and more profitable. They get the itch or nagging thought to give it a real go, aaanndd…. BAM! An agency is born.

However, most agency owners are swamped. Every. Single. Day. You wear many hats: owner, creative, development, fulfillment, sales, account service, accounting, and about a thousand other things. Even if you have a partner and several employees, as owner you juggle many responsibilities. You are super busy!

Busy is great, but if you're too busy to determine where you want

SYSTEM 1: CLARITY

to go, how will you ever get there? That's why it's crucial to set your company vision - whether you're just starting out or have been established for a while - it is never too late.

Your vision is your destination. It gives you some clarity on where you're heading. It's not only important you have that clarity, but also that you communicate it with your team. If your employees understand the big picture they are more likely to help you create the vision. When there is no clear vision, employees are more likely to make decisions based on what's best for them instead of what's best for the business simply because they don't know any better. Set your destination now so you can map the course and begin the journey.

Sharing your vision also creates synergy between leadership and employees. Generally speaking, productivity and output is better when people understand it and believe in it. Your team's motivation, attitude, and mood will be benefit from you sharing your vision.

Lesson 1.1: Defining A Clear Path

*It is the leader who's responsible for creating and communicating the company vision clearly through **words, data, and passion**.*

First things first. **What do you want?**

The law of attraction causes us to attract the things we are thinking about into our lives. So it's important to know what you want so you can attract it.

Use this simple exercise to get clear. Place what you DO want in your business inside the circle. Place what you DON'T want outside of the circle. This will help you focus on what is important for you to have in your vision and goals.

With a clear picture of what you do and do not want in your business, you can now start to focus on the various categories in your business and determine what's going to help you get there.

When creating your vision you'll want to consider the following seven elements:

1. Financial: This is where you're going to set your agency's financial goals. Where do you want to be, in financial terms, in the next year? What about in two years? Focus on absolutes, like bottom line profitability and year over year growth, etc. Be specific with actual dollar figures and percentages. Unless you're running at an ideal profit margin (10-15%), you shouldn't tie your financial goals to gross revenue. Gross doesn't mean squat if you've got profit leaks. (More on that in System 8, but no skipping ahead!)

2. Market Position: Determine where you want your agency to be in relation to the market. Do you want to be a leader or a follower? You might think "leader" is the right answer but honestly, there is no single right or wrong answer. If you aren't comfortable positioning yourself as an industry leader, you might prefer to let other agencies lead so you can model what they're doing, tweak it, and make it your

SYSTEM 1: CLARITY

own. You can modify your vision and let it evolve as your agency grows. Your answers to these questions may be different today than they are in a year, or five years from now.

3. Business Areas: Identify the businesses that you want to be in, and ones you do not want to be in. Think about what types of projects excite you and what types don't appeal to you. What types of brands do you love working on and which bore you? Don't just think about making money here but be very honest with yourself about what brands, industries, or projects you would love to work with, and which you would love to turn down if you could.

4. Innovation: Do you want to be first in the market with a new product or service? Or do to let others do the innovating and your agency adapts accordingly? Choosing not to be an innovator isn't necessarily a bad thing.

Today, Apple is considered one of the leaders in technology and innovation. However, that wasn't always the case. For example, they were not on the forefront of portable digital music players (MP3 players). Steve Jobs called gadgets like those "crap" and everyone at Apple agreed. Even though MP3 players had been around since the mid-1990's, Apple found all of them offered a less than stellar user experience. It wasn't until late 2001 that Apple rolled out the original iPod. One could argue that taking this one piece of technology and improving upon it changed the course of Apple's business forever.

Cautiousness is not a fault, even in a creative industry like advertising; first is not always best.

5. Insider Perception: How do you want to be perceived by your employees? This includes things like, their perception of your leadership style, work ethic, values and principles. Be honest and specific in how you want insiders to perceive you. It can be really difficult to look inward and evaluate yourself at this level but it's important to reflect upon who you are and whether it matches the perception you want to achieve. You'll use this insider perception as you develop your agency's core values a bit later in System 1.

6. Outsider Perception: The outside perception is probably the piece of your vision which will be the most difficult to harness. However, defining it is still an important piece in assembling your vision and clarity. How do you want outsiders to perceive your business? Things like culture and style shape the outside perception of your agency. Is your agency a commodity or a resourceful advisor? You need to determine how you want outsiders to view your agency because this outside perception becomes your brand. What people think and say about you ultimately defines your brand. If they're going to form an opinion anyway, you may as well use it to your advantage.

7. Workforce Characteristics: What kind of people do you want working for you? Do you want experience? Other entrepreneurs? Innovators? Team players? Independent thinkers? And what traits are you looking for in your ideal employees? Consider things like: cautiousness, ambition, resourcefulness, reservedness, introvertedness. Maybe you want someone who is comfortable wearing many hats or someone who can do more with less. Do you want someone with experience in a specific software or who has a specific skill set? Identifying these characteristics before a hiring need arises keeps the guesswork to a minimum later on.

STEPS TO WRITING & SHARING YOUR VISION:

1- Writing the first draft of your vision.

Don't overthink it. Go with your gut. Be honest with yourself but also let yourself shoot for the stars. You're the only one who's going to see these notes, so go ahead and dream!

Writing a vision is hugely important, but don't let its perceived weightiness work against you. The amount of time you spend drafting it is, in my experience, unrelated to the quality of the vision. I would actually argue that the two are inversely related—those who just dive in and get something down on paper almost always are the ones who emerge from this process with the most creative and inspiring visions.

You can compose your vision in any style you like: prose or bullet points, handwritten or typed. I've even seen people draw it out and have someone take notes while they talk through their illustration.

The most important thing to do before you even start is to put the word DRAFT at the top of your document. I've found by simply writing the word at the top of the page, my clients get a lot more input. Without it, people tend to assume the vision is final and there's no point providing any real feedback. (More on seeking feedback a little later in this section.)

Before you start writing, let me provide a few technical tips. If you follow them, the result will be so much better:

- Go for something great.
- Write from the heart.
- Step into the future.
- Go quickly, ignoring typos or misspellings.
- Get personal.

Now, with all these rules in mind, and the vision elements above, find a quiet place where you can spend an uninterrupted 30 minutes to write your vision draft. When complete, set it aside for a few days. Go back to all the other stuff you do every day.

2- Review and rewrite the vision.

When you're ready to revise, read your draft through from start to finish. Don't erase anything. If you're on the computer, start the second round by copying your first file so you can edit what you wrote without losing the original version.

In my experience, at least 80% of what is in that first scary rendition is pretty much right on. In any case, you'll have plenty of opportunity to edit the content and the language. As you read through, keep in the back of your mind: Does this sound inspiring? Do I get excited when I'm reading it? (Remember, it can be exciting and scary all at the same time.)

How specific should you get? The more detail, the better. It helps make the vision more real. Stay away from vague statements like "We're busier than ever"; instead, use real sales numbers that mean something. Without definition, you will have no details on what success actually looks like.

Saying something like, "I want to be wealthy" is all well and good, but what one person defines as rich might be someone else's definition of slightly less poor. Spell it out. Don't shy away from being specific. What are the key financial numbers that define success for you? Do you have certain sales levels, salary, or status you'll reach? Include those numbers in your vision.

Along the same lines, a personal vision might be, "I spend a lot of time with my kids." That's nice, but I think you'll get a lot further with something like, "I spend two to three weeks a year traveling the country with my kids. It's amazing how much fun we have." Or, "One night a week I go out to dinner with my entire family and the kids each take turns choosing new restaurants to try." See the difference? You want to practically be able to see it… that's why it's called a vision :)

3- Solicit input.

This is where you let the cat out of the bag. Now's the time to share your revised vision with people you trust and respect. This is where having the word DRAFT at the top comes in useful. Take input and opinions constructively. If you're sharing this with the right people, their valuable input can have a real impact on helping your vision take shape. Revise as you see fit.

But remember this is your vision, and you're not obligated to change anything.

SYSTEM 1: CLARITY

4- Share the vision.

Once final, it's time to share the vision with everyone who will be involved in implementing it. Don't be hesitant. You need to own the vision for where your agency is headed. And, when you share the company vision you are not only paving a direction for your team, you're also empowering them to help achieve it.

When people don't understand where your company is headed they will run to you for answers or decisions. When they do know the path to where they're headed they're able to make decisions in the best interest of the company without you. When you aren't dragged into every decision, your time is freer to concentrate on growth-oriented responsibilities.

I will caution you, though, that when you roll out your vision to a bigger group, people will inevitably ask questions about how you intend to achieve it. They're asking you about the how. The vision, however, is the what. It's totally fine if you don't know how you're going to get there. You will figure it out. Success is a marathon, not a sprint.

CREATING YOUR CORE VALUES

Now that you have created your vision, you'll want to develop a set of core values that support the vision. You'll use your core values as a set of standards and criteria for deciding who you surround yourself with and how you'll handle business situations as they arise.

I know what you might be thinking. Core values are so cheesy. But true core values aren't just a bunch of hokie rules that sound clever or cute, they're the ones that are woven into every aspect of your business to set a tone, create culture, and support the vision of the company.

Zappos.com has long been highly acclaimed for their culture-shaping core values. They recruit, hire, train, and fire based on their core values.

Zappos.com CEO, Tony Hsieh, has said for the first several years, company leadership was pretty resistant to the idea of setting core values. Most core values are written like a press release or a formal marketing document given to people on their first day of work, or hung as a meaningless plaque on the wall.

What the leadership at Zappos.com wanted instead was a set of core values that were committable and actionable. They wanted a set of standards, independent of specific job responsibilities, which they would use as a basis to hire and fire by.

The approach Tony took was actually pretty unique. Instead of getting all the executives together at an offsite meeting to create their list of core values, he solicited suggestions from the entire company. He sent one email to the entire staff inviting input. From that, the management team created their list of ten core values:

1. Deliver WOW Through Service
2. Embrace and Drive Change
3. Create Fun and A Little Weirdness
4. Be Adventurous, Creative, and Open-Minded
5. Pursue Growth and Learning
6. Build Open and Honest Relationships With Communication
7. Build a Positive Team and Family Spirit
8. Do More With Less
9. Be Passionate and Determined
10. Be Humble

With the implementation of core values, Zappos.com operationalized them in order to define the company and determine vision. Having core values in place has also defined their culture. They hire based on these very core values and every one of the them is touched upon in their behavioral interview technique. Sample questions include things like:

SYSTEM 1: CLARITY

- **Core Value #1** - *"Tell a story of a great customer service experience you've had."*

    If someone can't identify a positive customer service experience, they probably can't deliver one either. However, if they can share a great story they'll be able to "deliver the WOW."

- **Core Value #3** - *"If you could choose a theme song to play every time you walk into the room, what would it be and why?"*

    There's no wrong answer here, the interviewer just wants to see that the candidate can answer it with a sense of humor. Silliness is key if someone is going to "create fun" at work.

- **Core Value #4** - *"On a scale of 1-10, how lucky are you?"*

    The thought behind this question is that luck is not an inherent trait. It's more about being open to the possibility of luckiness. So, if someone answers a 10 or a 1 on the scale the candidate is probably not open-minded enough to embody the values of adventure, creativity and open-mindedness.

These are just a few examples of how Zappos.com utilizes their core values. And it goes beyond behavioral interviews because they've also integrated their core values into their daily operations, too:

- **Core Value #1** - Instead of spending a ton of money on advertising, Zappos.com invests more to deliver an amazing customer experience. They offer free-shipping both ways, a one-year return policy, surprise overnight shipping, and run a 24-hour warehouse for order fulfillment. These costly enhancements help "Deliver WOW Through Service" and translates into more than 70% of their business being from repeat customers.

- **Core Value #6** - The All Hands Meeting is Zappos.com's quarterly company-wide meeting. The entire company shuts down to attend this meeting and hear updates, ask questions, and celebrate wins. This isn't just for employees, either. The meetings are streamed live online, so vendors, investors and customers can all be part of it.

- **Core Value #7** - They do not focus on work/life separation, instead they encourage employees to be the same person at home and at work. They believe in work/life integration and have found this makes their team happier, results in better work, and allows for true work friendships to develop.

At Zappos.com the company vision is clear and focused. Employees believe in what they're doing and have a set of standards to help them make their decisions every day. They make decisions based on what's best for the company and with a growth mentality.

It's OK if you don't have company vision in place from day one. A lot of us don't - myself included. My agency went many years without real clarity and in hindsight that was the source of many issues, the least of which being cash flow.

When I got really clear and communicated my vision with my team, the agency grew steadily, eventually making its way on to Atlanta's Top 25 Small Businesses lists for several consecutive years. We held similar honors on many other "Top" and "Best of" lists throughout the years. (Frankly these are the only "agency awards" I find to be valuable. I don't think creative awards win you clients or do much else for business growth.) However, we were proud to boast being one of the best places to work and that itself drew top talent to our agency. It also gave our existing employees a sense of pride, knowing they worked with someone on "that" list. We scored some great projects with some really high profile clients, which led to even bigger projects with even bigger clients - like: LegalZoom, Hitachi and Lotus Cars, all of which I attribute to having clear sight of our agency vision, communicating the vision from the top down, and living our core values on a daily basis.

SYSTEM 1: CLARITY

By communicating all of this and aligning it with our actions and directives, our team was able to understand their purpose and the impact of the role they played in the long term trajectory of the business. It empowered employees to act in the best interest of the agency, in order to execute the agency's vision. By evenly distributing the weight and empowering our team, my partner and I were able to concentrate on growing the business. When the agency leader(s) are tied to all the decision-making, it ultimately stands in the way of giving time and attention to areas which can grow the business.

Lesson 1.2: Creating a 90-Day Action Plan

When it is obvious the goals cannot be reached don't adjust the goals, adjust the actions.

Most people claim they understand the importance of goal setting and planning but the reality is, depending on the source, 65-80% of people never set goals. That figure is lower for those of us in business or entrepreneurial pursuits which promote goal setting and some degree of planning.

Unfortunately, though, statistics indicate that for those of us who *are* setting goals, roughly 70% fail to achieve them. To me, it's completely understandable that most people don't set goals when there's such a large margin for being unsuccessful. Besides, running an agency is HARD. agency owners get pulled in so many directions - wearing many hats, putting out many fires. Everything seems pressing, urgent, and important. How can one possibly achieve long term goals when you can't even make it through your email inbox every day?

With that said, I'm a big advocate of setting 90-day goals, instead of just annual goals. Let's be honest; it's very easy to set lofty goals in January, but being human, it's easy to fall of the wagon by, like, March. Ninety-day plans can keep momentum going and allow you to adjust your course if things aren't going in the right direction.

Ninety-day goals are also great for keeping your team engaged and motivated. You probably have quarterly meetings with them (and if not, you should!). Not only does a 90-day plan summarize your goals, it aids with trimming them into bite-sized tasks that can be listed, delegated, scheduled, and completed. That's why 90-day goals aren't just for you - they're for your team and even your contractors, too. What a great way to keep the team informed and inspired!

In this lesson you are going to set goals and implement a 90-day plan. You'll find a 90-day goal setting approach greatly increases your chances for success. And with success, creates a chain reaction of new goals set and additional successes.

When determining your goals, keep them short, concise, and specific. The three keys to achieving success on your 90-days goals are to keep them written, time bound, and measurable. These elements are important because:

- Productivity studies tell us most people can't focus on more than 5-7 things are once. **Keep your list of goals concise.** You'll want to make your list of 90-days goals a short one. In fact, you'll see below that I recommend just 3 goal categories: Financial, Time, and Creative. For extra motivation write them on a notecard and hang it in your office or mirror..

- In order for you to achieve your goals you need to write them using language that indicates activity. **Keep your goals actionable.** Use words like "create," "achieve," "develop," "finalize," "implement," etc. to help you visualize completion of your goals.

- **Be certain results are measurable.** Did you or did you not achieve your 90-day goals in 90-days time? You cannot accurately assess yourself or your team, unless your goals are specific and measurable. If your goals weren't achieved in 90-days, you can learn and adjust the goals for the next 90 day period.

SYSTEM 1: CLARITY

DETERMINING YOUR SHORT TERM GOALS

You must have clear goals to aim for in the next 90 days. With the end in mind, consider your goals in terms of three different types: Financial, Time, and Creative.

1. "Financial" Goal - Where do you want revenue to be in the next 90 days? Pick an actual number - a number that feels a little uncomfortable. If it already feels like you're going to attain it, you're not pushing yourself hard enough. Choosing something safe won't have any impact on you, your team, or your agency. In other words, don't take the easy way out.

2. "Time-Oriented" Goal - What do you wish you had time to do in your business? Maybe you wish you were able to spend one day per week working on the business instead of in the business. That is a great time goal. Select something that is important to you now but generally isn't getting done because outside obstacles stand in your way. Time management is an integral part of your planning process. It helps ensure each subgoal can be accomplished in the time frame which you decide.

3. "Creative" Goal - What does your agency need that will help it run smoother? There's always that thing (or several things) you know you need but never get around to doing, creating, or implementing. It might be a lead generation system, new client on boarding process, or even team building. Whatever it is that has been nagging at you, set a 90-day goal to get it done. The mission of your "creativity" goal is to put something into motion that will grow and scale your agency. (Hint: it could be as simple as implementing the 8 Systems in this book. Break it down to one System per week for 8 weeks and you're there in less than 90-days!)

DEVELOPING THE STRATEGY TO ACHIEVE YOUR GOALS

So, you've created a great list of 90-day goals. Print it or write it down. Tape it to your mirror or pin it to your bulletin board. As you're moving through your day, ask yourself if the tasks you're tackling are getting you closer to those goals. If not, think about ways to eliminate or delegate it. This takes lots of patience and practice; it means a change in behavior and perhaps a new look at your daily and weekly priorities.

The problem is what you're doing when you're not doing what you're supposed to be doing.

You should have 2-4 strategies per goal; this will serve as your compass and help pave your way. Once you have strategies listed it's time to determine which tasks will get you there. List out anywhere from 5-25 tasks that serve each strategy. Your final list will look something like this:

- **Financial Goal (state a specific goal)**
  ○ Strategy 1 (indicate a specific strategy)
    - Task 1 (indicate specific task)
    - Task 2
    - Task 3
    - Task 4
    - Task 5
  ○ Strategy 2
    - Task 1
    - Task 2
    - Task 3
    - Task 4
    - Task 5

And so on, for each of the 3 goals (Financial, Time-Oriented, and Creativity).

In your mind, you must separate the things that you think are most urgent (checking emails) with the things that are most important (like creating a lead generation system). The late Dr. Stephen Covey,

SYSTEM 1: CLARITY

was one of the world's foremost leadership authorities. He was also a teacher, speaker, author and advocate for leading a principle-centered life. As a thought leader in his industry, he always believed "you have to decide what your highest priorities are and have the courage—pleasantly, smilingly, nonapologetically, to say 'no' to other things. And the way you do that is by having a bigger 'yes' burning inside. The enemy of the 'best' is often the 'good'."

One of Dr. Covey's most famous analogies is about prioritizing your life with "big rocks" first, focusing on health, marriage, and family as the big rocks. After those priorities, fill your time with smaller rocks, pebbles and sand which symbolize things in life that come up along the way. Dr. Covey asks you to imagine a mason jar. You have big rocks, small rocks pebbles, and sand. If you fill the jar first with the smaller items there's no room for the big rocks. However, if you insert the big rocks first you can backfill with the smaller items. In this analogy your life is the mason jar and you decide how to fill it. Big rocks first. This is sound advice for meeting your professional goals, as well. Your role within your business is the mason jar. Big rocks first.

So, set a strategy and stick to it. Make a list of all the things you need to do and rank them in order of impact. Start with big impact long term items, big impact short term items, average impact items, and finally, low impact items. When you prioritize your task list based on impact and the importance it plays in your long term goals you get a clearer understanding of what you should be doing. Unfortunately the mistake a lot of people make is doing the low impact items first - those are the easy things that are easily checked off your 'to do' list. Getting those things done gives us a sense of accomplishment and immediate gratification. However, a more effective plan of attack is to start with the big impact first. Fill your time with the things that are going to have long term, biggest impact on your agency. Then trickle in some of the small stuff.

In the spirit of Dr. Covey, I'm stressing to you - DO NOT let good get in the way of best. Think of the bigger picture. Say 'no' to all the things that hinder you from achieving your goals. (Easier said than done, I know!) Think about it from an objective standpoint. It all needs to get done, but it all doesn't need to get done by you. Like most other business decisions, it comes down to opportunity cost. What is it costing you not to achieve your goals?

ACCOUNTABILITY FOR 90-DAY GOALS

"Obstacles are what you see when you take your eyes off of the goal."
~ Vince Lombardi

Remember, the significance of creating 90-day goals is that you can check in to measure and adjust your course quicker. With annual goals, we often forget to step back to analyze or evaluate things until the eleventh month. Any changes at that point are typically too little, too late. With quarterly, 90-day goals you are able to measure in shorter increments, leaving time to evaluate, adjust and execute differently. If you set goals and don't measure them regularly you might be setting yourself up for disappointment.

So, at the 90-day mark, it's time to assess where you're at, how you did at implementing your strategy and whether you've achieved your goals. This should be a fairly quick and easy assessment because your goals were **time bound** and **measurable**. Use your assessment as a springboard to create new 90-day goals and repeat the process every single quarter. It takes some discipline, but it's worth it as you see results more rapidly.

SYSTEM 1: CLARITY

Recap: System 1 - Clarity

Every business needs the proper foundation on which to build. System 1 is about establishing a company vision and defining the path that leads to the vision.

▶ **Lesson 1.1: Defining A Clear Path**

One of the most important yet often overlooked pieces to building a successful business is having a clear vision. Your vision is your destination and you must know where you're headed so you can plan your travel route.

The best way to craft a company vision is by first defining what you do and do not want in your business. There are 7 elements to consider when crafting a vision:

1. Financial Goals
2. Market Position
3. Business Areas
4. Innovation
5. Insider Perception
6. Outsider Perception
7. Workforce Characteristics

Once you've drafted a vision and invited suggestions/comments from a few trusted sources, you must share your final draft with your team. Even if you don't have all the details fleshed out, it's important that your employees know and understand the long term direction of what they're helping build.

You may also decide to develop some core values that support the company vision. This will help you and your team decide how you do business and with whom. The best, most successful core values are woven into your daily business practices.

ACCELERATING YOUR AGENCY

▶ Lesson 1.2: Creating a 90-Day Action Plan

A lot of people set annual goals however, I advise setting 90-day goals. With smaller goals and a shorter chunk of time, it's easier to achieve them and keep the momentum going.

When determining your 90-day goals keep them short, concise and specific. The three keys to achieving success on your 90-days goals are to keep them *written, time bound,* and *measurable*. You should have one goal in each of 3 categories:

1. **Financial Goal** - a specific revenue or margin to reach. Don't go for the sure thing; make it a number that seems a little uncomfortable.

2. **Time-Oriented Goal** - select something that is important but generally isn't getting done because you don't have time to do it then decide how you can manage your time differently to achieve it.

3. **Creativity Goal** - think of something that would help your agency run smoother and get you closer to your vision then decide to create it and implement.

Next, create a 90-day action plan for achieving each goal. The action plan should consist of the strategies and specific tasks that will help you achieve each of the three 90-day goals. You'll use this action plan to help you decide what you should and should not be spending time on in your daily activities. And, since you're working on 90-day goals instead of annual goals you'll know that much sooner if you're headed in the wrong direction. So you can change focus and reset yourself on the right track.

Get more tools, instructional videos, and agency document templates at TheAgencyPlaybook.com

SYSTEM 2

Positioning

If you describe your agency as "full service," chances are you are losing business. If you find yourself having a hard time explaining what you do or skirting around the answer when asked what your agency does, you are losing opportunities.

In this chapter, you'll learn:

1. The benefits of choosing a niche and specialization.
2. How to determine who you will and will not work with.
3. The tactics you can implement to position your agency as an authority.

I strongly believe the reason my agency landed big clients like Legal Zoom, Hitachi, and AT&T was because we defined a specialization. Before we identified ourselves as specialists, we were lumped together with all the other generalists. However, we became the absolute best at one thing and marketed ourselves that way. Our specialization created a buzz which resulted in big brands like these and others chasing after us. There's an avalanche effect when this occurs. Being viewed as an expert within a specialty also allowed us to charge a premium for our services.

In this system you are going to define your ideal client and position yourself as the leading expert. In a sea of agencies, you will position yourself as "the choice" rather than "a choice." Once you have focus on who you want to work with and, equally important, an understanding of who you do not want to work with - you can direct your marketing to a specific target. By understanding their challenges, empathizing with their struggles, providing goodwill and demonstrating value you will be viewed as an authority. You will be sought after as their trusted advisor instead of just a commodity or an order-taker.

SYSTEM 2: POSITIONING

Lesson 2.1: Identifying Your Niche & Specialization

You still can do work outside of your niche, you're just not directing your marketing at it.

One of the big mistakes marketers today make is the "spray and pray method." They go after a very broad and undefined market. This approach leaves them with a weak, diluted message that is void of real substance. This is a generalist's approach which does not build authority and can be a turnoff to the big clients they're hoping to attract.

When you specialize in a particular industry or skill set, you become drastically more knowledgeable than your competitors. You are also able to provide direction and insights that your competitors cannot. You learn the nuances of that particular niche, including their special language and the details of their ideal clients. If you specialize in a specific skill set or become the masters of a specific technology you're able to become more efficient than your competitors. And, you're able to create strategic partnerships that your competitors cannot.

Now I know you might be thinking that you're a full service agency and you really can do everything. Why would you ever declare a niche when your possibilities are endless? To that I call B.S. Frankly, if you are a jack-of-all-trades, it means you are the master of none.

One of the biggest reasons agency owners are hesitant to choose a niche is because they're afraid they will be pigeon-holed and miss out on potential opportunities. Truthfully, the opposite is true. The fact is, agencies are missing out if they do not select a niche. Clients don't want a "me too agency"; they want an agency that is the very best at what they do.

Think of it this way: if you were going to be compensated on results alone, what service or industry would you choose? There are three ways you can identify a specialization for your agency. Chances are, you already have specialization - you just don't realize it yet!

Consider niching in:

1. one specific industry (vertical niche),
2. one specific technology or unique service (horizontal niche) or
3. a combination of both (vertical and horizontal).

Let's use Mark Zuckerberg's marketing approach for Facebook as an example. At its inception in early 2004, (the) Facebook was just for students of Harvard. Within a couple months it was rolled out to include other university students, eventually Facebook was opened to anyone with a .edu email address. In late 2005, Facebook expanded to high school students, and… well, you get the picture. The genius behind this framework is to master one market before taking on another. Speak their language. Help them, serve them, and then grow into another niche.

When you serve a specific market you have the opportunity to earn the reputation of an expert. Selecting a niche doesn't necessarily mean you have to turn down other work. It simply means you direct your marketing to one market - you build trust and authority, all the while gathering case studies and testimonials that continue to build your reputation.

1. DETERMINING YOUR VERTICAL

The absolute best way to determine a vertical niche is to take a close look at your existing success stories. What types of industries do you enjoy helping? What are you most knowledgeable about and why? What drives your best work and what are you passionate about? Search for those answers and you'll find an inspiring niche right under your nose.

Drill down, get super specific. You want to really focus on a particular niche - let's say you're currently going after small businesses.

That's not specific enough. You'll actually want to go through my exercise and determine *which* small businesses. When you're really honest with yourself and you set aside your fear of niching, you'll find it pretty easy to identify your vertical.

So for example, instead of thinking "we serve small businesses," you'll consider your past experiences -- your knowledge, expertise, big wins, and major results -- and narrow it down to *small service based businesses*. Then, get even more specific to one type of service-based business, such plumbers. In this case, you'd market your agency as the marketing experts specializing in **marketing for the plumbing service industry**.

This is a vertical niche. By identifying a niche, you can use industry-specific phrases in your marketing so your prospects feel like you "get" them - you understand their business and you are the expert they should choose to help them solve their problem. Above all, identifying a niche allows you to truly understand your clients' business challenges, which can be used as leverage to make a sales.

It can be scary when you get this laser focused on a niche but it's worth it. When you are this specific and you become an industry leader, clients will seek you out instead of the other way around.

2. DETERMINING YOUR HORIZONTAL

It's tempting to market yourself as the agency who can DO all things, BE all things. Let's be honest. You can't possibly do all things well. You need to make a name and reputation for yourself as the best at something specific. If your agency has a unique, marketable technical skill or a ton of experience with a tool or software that is just now emerging in the advertising landscape, use this to your advantage and declare it as your agency's horizontal niche.

For example, if you're a digital agency - don't label yourself as a "digital agency." You can either define yourself as a digital agency to a specific industry (above) by identifying a vertical, or define a specific skill set or emerging technology as your horizontal niche.

Therefore, instead of just marketing yourself as a digital agency, be more specific and declare what type of digital marketing, such as SEO. Then, drill down even further to commit to SEO for lead generation. You can even take it step further and declare expertise in a specific technology or software tool. You'd market your agency as the digital marketing experts specializing in *SEO using (fill in the blank) for lead generation.*

3. DEFINING BOTH VERTICAL & HORIZONTAL NICHES

Under the right circumstances, your agency might do best by defining a combination of both an industry and a skill set. By declaring both a horizontal and vertical niche you are being extremely clear on exactly what you do and who you help. Marketing in this manner translates to a very clear purpose and intention. You can identify with very specific desires and challenges your prospects face and you'll have a very specific target for all your goodwill content. You'll no longer be generating generic blog posts, videos or social content as a catch-all. When your target audience searches key phrases specific to their industry, they'll find you and you'll be waiting to serve them.

Let's assume you're following the thought process for the vertical niche example above, which was: *experts specializing in marketing for the plumbing service industry.*

And then, also applying the horizontal niche from above, *experts specializing in SEO for lead generation.*

The end result, for a really focused positioning with both a vertical and horizontal, would be: *SEO Agency for the plumbing service industry specializing in lead generation.*

Don't let this scare you! There's no such thing as being "too specific." This positioning strategy will establish authority, build your reputation, and attract the right clients. And, because you're niching down to something you're good at and passionate about you'll deliver amazing results.

And again, you can still take on work outside your niche/specialization. You're just targeting your marketing to this audience as a way of narrowing down your focus. No more "spray and pray" method!

Lesson 2.2: Positioning as "The Choice" Rather Than "A Choice"

You'll be chosen over the competition when you make the story about them, not you. Be there to help and guide; let them be the hero of their own story.

Positioning is the way your agency is described and identified to the outside world. It's the way you communicate what you do and how you do it. When done correctly, it's one of the things that will give you an edge over your competition. With a very narrow niche defined you can now determine the best way to position yourself in the marketplace. You want to set your agency apart from all other agencies. You want to be considered THE choice, instead of just A choice.

In order to adequately position your agency, it's likely you'll need to change the way you think about what you're doing. Agency websites (and most service-oriented business sites) talk about who they are and what they do. They might include impressive lists and awards, talk a lot about themselves, their skills, their special certifications or trainings. That's not going to resonate with prospective clients.

Have you noticed, I often write that you are "helping" your clients or "serving" your clients? The word choice is intentional because that's exactly how your position should identify your agency. In a service industry, you are in existence to serve - not save. You are not the hero of your client's story. No one ever wants to feel like they need rescued.

There is a paradigm shift that needs to occur. For decades, agencies have positioned themselves as heroes who save the clients in distress.

The client might be in need of sales, customers, branding... whatever the case may be. That's when the superhero agency enters the picture with superhero cape billowing in the wind, standing tall to serve and protect the lost, suffering and feeble... The problem is, this superhero approach isn't working! Clients don't want to be saved, they want to be served.

That is why I have my clients create a Positioning Script which paints the client as the hero and the agency as their trusted advisor.

When considering your agency's Positioning Script think of ways you can make it all about them, the client. If your Positioning Script is all about you, the client will view you as a commodity. When their specific need is met, you'll be discarded. When you are *helping* or *serving* their needs, the relationship has room to grow and evolve. Your role is that of an adviser rather a hero that accomplishes one goal for them or solves one problem of theirs. If all your marketing points to you being the hero who eliminates their problems and saves the day, where does that leave the client? Just the damsel in distress or the hero's sidekick...

Think about it. With the agency-superhero approach, you're like Batman and the client is his sidekick, Robin. Unfortunately, Robin's wardrobe includes weird green tights. No one wants to wear green tights. Am I right? But, I digress...

Instead, think of your agency as a trusted advisor. Set up your client as the hero and you in the support role. When you shift your thinking, the client is Batman and your agency is Alfred. (By the way, who doesn't absolutely *love* Alfred?) He's dependable, trustworthy, wise AND Batman could never make it without him. (Sadly, he never gets to drive the Batmobile or kiss the girl, but he's super cool nonetheless.)

In the trusted advisor role, you need to know and demonstrate four key points:

SYSTEM 2: POSITIONING

1. You have empathy and an understanding of the hero's (client) current situation.
2. You have the unwavering authority and are the utmost qualified to help the hero (client).
3. You hold the hero (client) accountable for taking action in order to accomplish what they want.
4. You have a plan for helping the hero (client) have a successful ending to their story.

One brand who's nailed it with their positioning is Apple. Their entire positioning statement is centered around their products being a means for users to create beautiful things. The focus is on how Apple products helps the user (hero) make music, take photos, etc. The consumer is the hero - Apple is the trusted advisor.

When Apple launched the first iPod, Steve Jobs rolled it out with a simple phrase: "a thousand songs in your pocket." WOW! What a powerful statement! Steve didn't launch into details about all the product features and capabilities. Instead, he made it simple and easy to understand with a plain statement. Most often the buyer just wants to know one thing: *"what's in it for me?"*

WRITING A POSITIONING SCRIPT

In order to initiate a shift in mindset, I've developed an exercise to help you determine your position and to stand out as the choice. When you follow this specific framework, you can start writing the story of your agency's point of differentiation.

This framework is applicable to any service-based business. Therefore, I've included examples below of the way I would answer these questions for my coaching business.

1. **What does your client WANT?** Sure there's the one obvious thing - they want more sales. However, really zero-in on their business goals and desires. Consider things like: repeat business, lead generation, site traffic, etc. Make a list of 5-6 wants and

desires your ideal clients have; then pick the best one to use right now and hang onto the rest for later. (We'll return to this list for executing marketing campaigns in System 4.)

EXAMPLE: *My clients are agencies that want to grow their business bigger and faster.*

2. **What are your client's PROBLEMS?** What external issues do your clients face? Think about your common obstacles and your clients pain points. List 5-10 things holding them back from their wants and desires; then pick the most important one that you will help them tackle.

EXAMPLE: *My clients lack the knowledge and support to grow their agency.*

3. **How does your client FEEL about the problem above?** People shop for practical reasons (like filling a need or a want) but they actually make their buying decisions based on emotions and feelings. Combine your knowledge of your client's wants and their problems to list out a few of emotions you'd expect from your prospective clients.

EXAMPLE: *My clients feel doubtful, unclear, isolated, alone, and overwhelmed.*

4. **How can you EMPATHIZE?** As a trusted advisor, you need to be able to demonstrate empathy toward your client's situation. You have to demonstrate that you relate first hand or have worked with enough similar clients to have empathy. Have you been in their shoes, like I have been in your shoes having run my own agency for 12 years? List all the ways you understand your prospects' challenges and identify with their problems.

EXAMPLE: *I understand their struggles and where they want to take their agency.*

SYSTEM 2: POSITIONING

5. **How can you show AUTHORITY?** Communicating this key point is imperative. Your Positioning Script must tell your prospects what sets you apart from other agencies. What qualifies you as an authority to this specific target marketing? Perhaps you have success stories that can demonstrate your authority. Maybe you have partnered with or been certified by an industry-specific software tool. These things and more can establish and build your authority. (This is the only part of the Positioning Script that is about you, so let's make it a good list!)

    EXAMPLE: *I've helped over 10,000 agencies in 23 countries.*

6. **What is the PLAN?** How can you help or guide your client to a solution? Now that you've identified and empathized with their problems and demonstrated authority what actions do you recommend to them? Craft a line about your agency's detailed process or unique methodology.

    EXAMPLE: *I created the Agency Playbook that is broken down into eight systems.*

7. **What is the CALL TO ACTION?** This is where you plainly state the next step. You're putting the ball in the prospect's court, so what do they need to do with it? There are two types of CTA's: Direct (such as "buy now") and Transitional (such as "sign up" or "opt-in now"). You can offer one or both but be specific on what the client needs to do next in order to receive your help.

    EXAMPLE: *Opt-in by giving me their email address to learn more.*

8. **What's the picture of SUCCESS?** Look ahead to the client's future. How does life improve after they work with you? Consider both outward business-oriented successes (increased sales, site traffic, etc.), as well as inward personal successes (free time, sense of accomplishment, ending frustration, etc.) List 8-10 benefits they'll enjoy with their success and pull out the best 1-2.

EXAMPLE: *The client has increased revenue and experiences agency growth.*

9. **What's the TRAGIC RESULT?** Describe the client's consequences you're trying to avoid by helping them. What will happen if the client does not work with you? List 8-10 potential scenarios and use the top 1-2.

EXAMPLE: *The client could experience missed sale opportunities, losing to their competition, and a stalled business.*

After answering these nine questions put it all together to write a compelling story. This is your Positioning Script and it's how you will frame yourself as the Alfred and the client as Batman. Using your own language and voice, follow this formula for writing your Positioning Scrip:

Do you [WANT], but are struggling with [PROBLEM] which makes you [FEEL]?

We [EMPATHIZE] and have [AUTHORITY] to execute [PLAN] that shows you [SUCCESS] and avoid [TRAGIC RESULT].

This is your new Positioning Script. Remember, you want to set up the hero for success. You're just the Alfred - wise, dependable, trustworthy - but never gets to drive the Batmobile.

Lesson 2.3: Crafting an Elevator Pitch

Most of us have a really hard time explaining what we do but a casual, yet scripted, Elevator Pitch can change that and bring us new opportunities.

Imagine you run into an old colleague in a crowded shopping mall. You haven't seen him in years but you know he's still in the business. After the usual small talk, he asks, "Who are you working for these days?" You open your mouth to speak - you want to tell him you went out on your own and loving it. You know you need to spread the word but you can't even *find* the words much less spread them. What you do is so complex; where do you start? Then his wife is pulling him off in a different direction and before you can compose your thoughts, he's gone.

If you had been better prepared in this scenario, you might have a reason to cross paths or even do business together again. Perhaps this old colleague is client side now or knows someone who needs to connect with your agency. You'll never know because you fumbled. It's a lost opportunity for sure.

If this sounds familiar, you are not alone. A lot of agency leaders don't know how to describe what they do which ultimately has a ripple effect with their team and associates. When people ask you what you do, and you say "it's complicated" or "I run an advertising agency" you are putting off the inquiry and potentially closing the door to new opportunities.

Saying "it's complicated" could be misconstrued as insulting, as if the person couldn't possibly understand what you do. If you generically answer with "I run an ad agency" images of Darrin from *Bewitched* or Don Draper from *Mad Men* pop in their heads which isn't even close to your reality. Regardless, neither answer gets to the point and answering this way could be costing you sales.

What you need is a good Elevator Pitch to inspire conversation. An Elevator Pitch is a brief, persuasive speech that you use to spark interest in your business. A good Elevator Pitch should last no longer than a short elevator ride... hence the name. It should be interesting, memorable, and succinct. It must also explain what your agency does and why it's unique. All in under 20 seconds!

ELEMENTS OF A GREAT ELEVATOR PITCH

A great Elevator Pitch is directly correlated to your Positioning Script and has these characteristics:

- **Simple** - Your pitch should be easily understood. Using everyday street language makes a more lasting impression than long, fancy words that people have to Google.

- **Relevant** - You want your pitch to describe why you do what you do, so you don't have to provide any further explanation. Using engaging, relatable phrases your pitch will display its relevancy.

- **Repeatable** - You aren't the only one who's going to use the Elevator Pitch, so it needs to be something your team will be able to repeat with ease; nothing too cumbersome to memorize. Remember: keep it simple.

- **Memorable** - Your goal is to leave a lasting impression. The average person needs to hear something up to six times in order to remember, so your Elevator Pitch must cut through the noise and clutter.

Simply put, if you can't explain what you sell, people don't know why they should buy. Therefore you can't make it too vague, nor should you make it too technical. Using industry-specific language is a surefire way to lose people's interest. (Boring!) Try not to let your closeness to the business interfere with the way you describe what you and your agency does. Use layman's terms and keep it simple:

DON'T SAY: "Our agency is the Adwords certified Google experts for attorneys and law practices who want to increase visibility online and in the marketplace."

DO SAY: "Our agency helps lawyers who are overpaying for marketing by providing strategies to increase their number of clients and cases."

See the difference? Using technical phrasing and terminology makes it sound clunky. Keep it simple and straightforward. It's a one liner that explains who and how you help.

WRITING YOUR ELEVATOR PITCH

Your Elevator Pitch is directly related to your Positioning Script. The formula for an amazing Elevator Pitch has three parts. You can use your brainstorming from the Positioning Script exercise to write a winning Elevator Pitch.

1. **Identify a problem:** A simply stated, very specific pain point for your client.

2. **Explain a plan:** A brief, easily understood, new idea to solve the problem.

3. **Describe the successful ending:** A boiled-down description of your core business.

When you've got these three elements nailed down, try plugging into a format similar to this one:

"We help [CLIENT/NICHE] with [PROBLEM] by [PLAN] in order to [SUCCESS]."

USING YOUR ELEVATOR PITCH

The thing about an awesome Elevator Pitch is that it just naturally rolls off the tongue. Easier said than done, I know. But you can get really good at reciting your Elevator Pitch. The best way is to rehearse it, of course. Write it, say it, repeat it ad nauseam. However you don't want to sound too rehearsed or pre-recorded. Have some animation and show some passion, while also showing some restraint - leave them wanting to know more. Get it to a point where it casually flows without any thought.

Next, share it with your team. The Elevator Pitch is one of the most important pieces of information you'll share with your employees, second only to the company vision of course. Your employees are your walking, talking billboards. Arm them with the phrasing in your Elevator Pitch so when they run into an old colleague or client, they won't just say "I'm working in advertising." You never know what new opportunities await.

Finally, roll your Elevator Pitch into all your marketing. Some version of it should be on every page of your website. Be sure to create fluid messaging from your site and all landing pages to social media accounts and other marketing vehicles.

Lesson 2.4: Agency Website Makeover

Ask a ton of questions and listen more than you speak, even on your website.

I think we can all agree the client-agency relationship is the key to success of your business. And, what's that old saying about first impressions? You never get a second chance at them, right? So, no matter how a prospective client stumbles upon your site; it's got to feel comfortable and familiar right off the bat. Your client is looking for evidence that you are the authority capable of helping them solve their problems, challenges or issues.

I've seen too many agencies get this wrong, so I've dedicated an entire lesson to helping agencies structure their website in a way that lands more business. The absolute #1 thing you have to do in order to make sure your agency's website makes the best first impression is to look at it from the prospect's vantage point.

So, why do so many agency websites suck?

Well, it reminds me of the shoemaker's children who are shoeless. Marketing agencies are rock stars at marketing for their clients, but marketing themselves? Not so much...

For starters, a lot of agency websites are too braggy. Too many agency websites are all about the agency's awards, client list, creative, team, and office locations. While those things are important, they aren't

SYSTEM 2: POSITIONING

front-and-center, Homepage important. They are more like half-way-down the "About Page" important. Below, I'll walk you through exactly where any (very limited) bragging should occur.

Another agency site killer is not being specific enough. I believe this is sometimes done intentionally because of a fear to commit to a specific niche or specialization. So, some agencies try to be just vague enough in their site copy that they appear to be full service. Conversely, I think some agencies are too close to what they do and their site is unintentionally vague. On these types of sites, the headlines are too vague or false assumptions are made about what the visitor does and doesn't already know.

Other sucky agency sites don't do anything to establish authority. Afraid of losing out on a potential opportunity, many agency sites don't commit to being especially awesome at any one specific skill. The site visitor often leaves feeling more confused or uncertain as to whether the agency is capable of solving their problems or meeting their needs. In this section, you'll learn about reorganizing your site to demonstrate relevance and authority. Hold onto your seat, because it may even involve deleting some site content.

Last but not least, the worst agency website sin is not having a call to action. The most important thing you can do for agency growth is to capture a prospective client's information (email, phone, etc.) We know people are super protective of their contact info but when you have something valuable to offer they'll gladly give it up. (More on this later.)

If you're guilty of any of this (and I'll bet any money you are!) then a website makeover is in order. This isn't something you'll accomplish in a day. Instead, I suggest making this one of your 90-day goals. It will take dedicated time and effort, ideally a large chunk of uninterrupted time either by you or someone on your team, to dissect your site based on the following guidelines. Some of these changes are simple while others can be rather cumbersome, depending on the state of your site. But, since you've already got the perfect Positioning Script and an amazing Elevator Pitch, this ought to be a piece of cake!

STEPS TO REVISING YOUR WEBSITE

1. Start with a compelling question.

Your agency's Homepage helps prospects decide how much time they're going to spend on your site. The key is to make a compelling case to keep them there right out of the gate. And that's why it's got to be about them - not you.

Think for a moment about your Elevator Pitch. It's simply stated, concise, direct, and demonstrates a successful ending. You can use your Elevator Pitch to inspire the headline for your Homepage. How can you turn the statement of your Elevator Pitch into a compelling question?

By asking your prospective client a question you're immediately changing the conversation to being about them instead of you. Sure, it's your website but the visitors are there for themselves. That's why it's important that your headline is phrased in question format - it's not about what you do, it is about how they feel or a problem they face.

You can take your Elevator Pitch, add in a feeling from your Positioning Script, and construct a question that turns the focus from you to them.

Your Elevator Pitch is something like:

"We help [CLIENT/NICHE] with [PROBLEM] by [PLAN] in order to [SUCCESS]."

Turn that into a question, something like this:

"Are you a [CLIENT/NICHE] [FEELING] because of [PROBLEM]?"

Then add a subhead that restates a version of your Elevator Pitch. This immediately tells your prospect you understand their challenges, empathize with their feelings, and have a plan to help them achieve a successful ending.

2. Rethink your pages.

Try keeping the number of pages in your header or menu to a minimum. You can create as many pages as you want but most should be kept hidden. Fewer menu choices are just more effective than having many choices which become confusing or overwhelming. The categories I usually suggest are:

- Home
- About
- Services
- Blog
- Contact

You can be as creative as you'd like with your page names as long as they're descriptive, simple and specific. I also like to suggest page names or menu options that are actionable. For example, instead of having a "Contact" page, a more actionable page name would be "Get Our Help" - see the difference?

3. Reorganize your blog posts.

There are a couple different steps in a blog reorganization. To be honest, depending on how long and how active you've been blogging, it could prove very time consuming. With that said, it's entirely possible for a blog reorg to drastically increase your site traffic.

First, it's necessary to do a general *quality check* to ensure all your site content is still relevant to the audience you serve. If you've got old, irrelevant, or outdated blog posts prospective clients will feel as if you aren't qualified to help them. Keeping old news on your blog portrays an archaic or detached image. Readers will think you either don't understand them or aren't on top of the marketing trends and innovation.

Since you've honed in on a niche and defined who your ideal client is, you've probably got some irrelevant content. If you've got outdated posts about technology that has changed, job postings that have been filled, or posts about tools or software that has evolved over time, it's time for a purge.

Depending on the age of your agency and the consistency in which you've been blogging, this has the potential to be a rather large task. As you look through your archived blog posts, consider rating them as follows:

- **Content to keep.** Keep all posts that are timeless and relevant to your niche/specialization.

- **Content to delete.** It's about quality, not quantity; eliminate all old, irrelevant, or boring posts.

- **Content to refresh.** You may find there are blog posts that are "OK" but could be better. Dedicate some time to refreshing those posts to breathe new life into them.

- **Content to consolidate.** If you've got multiple posts on the same topic, consolidate them into one epic post. (And, avoid confusion by doing a redirect to the new post.)

Whether you are keeping, refreshing, or consolidating, you want people to see your best stuff. Rewrite post titles to rank better, review, or add a call-to-action (because every post should have one!). Also check embedded links and reformat if needed.

Second but of equal importance is to thoughtfully and strategically *categorize your blog posts*. First-time site visitors are engaging with your site for a specific reason (and that reason is known only to them). Your goal is to make a great first impression right off the bat by providing value and demonstrating your authority. This doesn't mean be braggy - let your competitors' sites do that. Instead you want to fill your site with information to answer the visitors questions right away, and if you're lucky they'll peruse your site for awhile.

<u>Blog categories</u>: Think about why people are visiting your site. What problems do they hope you can fix? What desires do they hope you can fulfill? These are the blog content categories you should create. Also, consider your future content plans and the general direction your blog will take in the coming months and years. Begin creating a list of categories to correspond with what you have been and will be doing.

I advise jotting down all your initial category ideas and whittle the list down later. Try to find a few common themes among all your blog content. My suggestion is a minimum number of categories, like 4 or 5 max. Too many categories end up being confusing and overwhelming. Besides, if your posts require more than 4-5 categories you might be trying to cover too many topics. Think strategically about what your blogging goals and objectives are, then execute accordingly.

4. Revise your About Page.

Believe it or not, your About Page is not about you. Yes, really! Prospects find your site because they need something. They don't necessarily want to hear all about you but rather why you can provide what they need. Information about who you are is only secondary to how you can serve them.

Start your About Page by providing a statement - not a story - on what you do. Focus on them first by explaining what you do and how you do it. Select word choices that demonstrate your authority in their industry and why you're the best within your specialty.

Next, confirm for your prospects that they're in the right place.

Develop copy that shows the ways you understand their needs and struggles. List it in bullet form or craft a short paragraph. Similar to your Homepage, this can also be done in the form of questions and keeps the focus on the prospect.

Here's how I address coaching clients who visit my About Page:

Have you ever asked yourself:

"How the heck can I scale my agency?"

"Do I really have what it takes to grow?"

"I'm so burned out with running this agency."

"How can I generate more leads & stop relying on referrals?"

"How can I find time to do to work on the business and not in the business?"

"What systems do I need in place?"

"How do I position to sell my agency?"

You're in the RIGHT place!

Growing an agency is very difficult, because there is so much competition for clients and talent. You're frustrated and unclear what to do next. I spent over a decade developing the framework to grow, scale and eventually sell my agency. Today over 20,000 agencies in 42 countries have used it to do the same.

With affirmation that they're in the right place, then you can briefly describe your experience and credentials. This should be just one or two sentences to explain why you are experienced and qualified to deliver the goods or services your prospect needs/desires. The next couple sentences of copy should identify what separates your agency from the others and how else they can achieve their desired result.

So, if they've made it this far on your About Page the visitor actually does want to hear your story. Allow some space and then create a short section to tell the story about how and why the agency was founded, mission, goals, team, or leadership. It's fine to take a creative approach but keep it concise and relevant.

As you wrap up your About Page, include a call to action, such as an invitation to Like or Follow you on social media, as well as an opt-in to subscribe.

5. Every page needs a Call to Action.

Yes - Every. Single, Page. Need I say more? The CTA is the most important element of your site. You can use a combination of transitional and direct CTAs, but there's no excuse for not having something on every page.

We've all visited websites that have the generic "Join Our List" or "Sign Up For Our Newsletter" opt-in box. That doesn't really cut it if your want to use your website to grow your business. Instead, use something that touches upon solving a common problem or challenge your clients frequently face.

Inject the same language from your Positioning Script, such as: "Click to Learn More About [SUCCESS]" or "Want to Learn More About How We [PLAN]?" in order to make them raise their hand and accept additional marketing from you in the form of an opt-in.

FINALIZING YOUR WEBSITE MAKEOVER

Making these initial changes might seem like a daunting task. However, your agency website can be one of your best lead generators. Therefore it's important to give it the time and attention it deserves. Besides, your website should always be evolving and changing as you get a better grasp on your specialization/niche, ideal clients and their needs/wants. By making these adjustments now, you'll be further demonstrating why your agency is "the choice" rather than just "a choice."

Recap: System 2 - Positioning

Trying to be a jack-of-all-trades will leave you as the master of none. This section is about identifying your agency's strengths and area of expertise. Then, marketing those as benefits to the ideal clients who need those skills.

▶ **Lesson 2.1: Identifying Your Niche & Specialization**

One of the big mistakes marketers today make is the "spray and pray method" of marketing to a very broad and undefined audience. This generalist's approach leaves them with weak messaging void of any real substance. Instead of trying to be a jack-of-all-trades (yet master of none), declare a niche or specialization and get laser focused on being the best at one skill set or in one industry. There are 3 ways you can drill down your service offering:

1. Vertical niche: Select a specific industry your agency serves and market to them. A great way to identify a vertical niche is look back at your success stories and figure out what they have in common.

2. Horizontal niche: This means marketing your agency as the master of a specific skill set or software tool. You will build a reputation and be perceived as the leading authority of a specific area of advertising due to your agency's proficiency and results.

3. Vertical and horizontal niche: Coupling a defined industry and specific skill set, under the right circumstances, can be an extremely effective approach to niching down.

Remember, you are declaring a niche in order to concentrate your marketing message. However you can still work with other clients outside your niche.

▶ **Lesson 2.2: Positioning as "The Choice" Rather than "A Choice"**

SYSTEM 2: POSITIONING

Position your agency as Alfred, the trusted advisor. Let the client be Batman, the hero.

A Positioning Script will help you tell a compelling story in which your client can "see" themselves working with you. Use the 9 step exercise in System 2 to write your script following this formula:

Do you [WANT], but are struggling with [PROBLEM] which makes you [FEEL]?

We [EMPATHIZE] and have [AUTHORITY] to execute [PLAN] that shows you [SUCCESS] and avoid [TRAGIC RESULT].

▶ Lesson 2.3: Crafting an Elevator Pitch

A lot of agency owners have a hard time explaining what we do when in a casual setting. Too technical sounds robotic, too general sounds broad and can be misconstrued as an insult. The solution is preparing an Elevator Pitch to recite when an opportunities arise.

The 4 elements of a great Elevator Pitch are: simple, relevant, repeatable, and memorable. You can use the 3 part formula in System 2 to write an Elevator Pitch that looks something like this:

"We help [CLIENT/NICHE] with [PROBLEM] by [PLAN] in order to [SUCCESS]."

Then practice, practice, practice. Next, share it with your team and have them do the same. Finally roll your Elevator Pitch, or some form of it, into all your marketing.

▶ Lesson 2.4: Agency Website Makeover

Does your agency website suck? It might, and maybe you don't even realize it?! Here are a few rules to keep in mind for your agency website refresh:

DON'T:

- ... be too braggy on your website's homepage. You won't impress new clients with awards or achievements you've received for your past work. The "About Us" stuff does not belong front and center.
- ...leave old or irrelevant blog posts on your site. This is your only chance to make a first impression, so only keep your best stuff on there.
- ...confuse or over complicate what you do and how you do it. Using agency-speak or technical language is a turn off.

DO:

- ...make the site visitor the center of attention. Establish your authority by asking a question they're compelled to answer.
- ...clean up your blog posts by condensing duplicates and deleting irrelevant or outdated information, as well as organizing them into 4-5 categories.
- ...minimize the number of visible pages you have on your site with the homepage being focused entirely on your target audience. Use simple language to clearly empathize with their challenges and their desired outcomes.

Get more tools, instructional videos, and agency document templates at TheAgencyPlaybook.com

SYSTEM 3

3 Offering

ACCELERATING YOUR AGENCY

If you have a hard time landing big projects for your core service pay close attention to the lessons in this System. Having a service offering ladder in place, along with the proper pricing, will have a significant impact on your agency's revenue goals.

In this chapter, you'll learn:

1. How to determine your service offering ladder (and why having one is so important).
2. How to figure out what to charge in order to meet your agency's revenue goals.
3. Whether your pricing model should be based on hours, value, performance or a hybrid.

It's natural to want to sell your core service first. It's what your agency does best and it's your bread and butter. Core service projects typically have higher price tags and are longer engagements. Problem is, it's a huge commitment for your prospective clients which means it can be a really difficult decision for them. It's like proposing marriage on the first date. Who's ready to commit to something that huge so soon?

Having an accurately priced service offering ladder means a full pipeline, faster sales cycle, and increased agency revenue.

Lesson 3.1: Creating a Service Offering Ladder

Long term agency-client relationships aren't like speed dating; they require a courtship before proposing marriage.

So many agencies are doing it wrong (including mine, when I had one). Pitching the agency's core service right off the bat is a mistake. It's jumping ahead without establishing the know-like-trust factor. Proving your helpfulness and building a relationship of trust is going to land you far more business opportunities than a one-off, large ticket project.

SYSTEM 3: OFFERING

A Service Offering Ladder is a visual representation of all the services your agency offers. I like to tell my clients to work backwards when creating their ladder. What I mean by that is to think about your core service and then list out all the other services your agency provides, most of which are slices off the core.

Using the list you've brainstormed with your core service and the sliced off services you offer, you'll create something that resembles a step ladder. The idea is to keep your prospects engaged in increasingly larger, more frequent work with your agency rather just one large, one-time project.

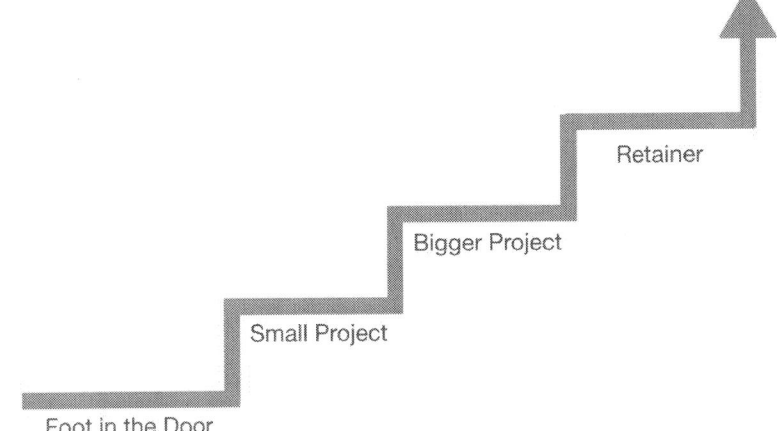

THE FOOT IN THE DOOR

Starting at the base level of the ladder is the Foot in the Door Offer. There are a variety of benefits to a Foot in the Door Offer done right.

- **It offers a low cost point of entry.** You'll find you actually make more money when you start small and have your clients stairstep their way up.

- **It's the courtship before the marriage.** It is a great way to get to know each other. You can build your authority and gain more trust, as well as get a glimpse of a client's workstyle, vision, and goals.

- **It helps determine what the client really wants.** It allows you to dig into their current landscape, see what's missing, and provide insight. It also prevents you from spinning your wheels on a larger project that might not be exactly what the client needs (just ends up being what they *think* they want).
- **It pre-qualifies your prospects.** By selling a Foot in the Door first, you'll get the opportunity to qualify your prospects. You can find out if they have the budget to work with you, as well as determine in advance if you can successfully help them.
- **It speeds up the sales cycle.** When you have a lower priced point of entry it's much easier for your prospects to make the decision to work with you. After you fulfill delivery and wow them with your expertise you'll find subsequent sales decisions are made much faster.
- **The likelihood of repeat business increases by 20X.** Depending on the source, once a client buys from you they are up to 20X more likely to buy again in the future because they already know, like, and trust you.

What makes a great Foot in the Door Offer?

First and foremost, bear in mind that you will not make money on a Foot in the Door Offer. That's not the goal at all. Instead of making money from it, though, you'll experience exponential growth in revenue and profits by the increased business it brings. The goal of a successful Foot in the Door Offer is to build your agency business and move prospects through your service offering ladder.

It needs to be super simple. Make sure you are managing expectations as to what your prospect is getting from the Foot in the Door Offer. Call it a discovery, blueprint, paid consultation… Just be certain it's something you can explain pretty easily.

The process for proposing and delivering a Foot in the Door Offer should be pretty turnkey. No fancy, lengthy proposal necessary. A one or two page sales sheet should explain the timeline, process, deliverables, and price.

SYSTEM 3: OFFERING

One common mistake I see a lot of agency owners making with their Foot in the Door is over delivering. Most are already doing free consultations (which I highly discourage) so the first time they do provide low cost initial engagement in lieu of a consultation they feel the need to give away an abundance of information in order to justify charging for it. In fact, one of my clients actually did so much work on their first Foot in the Door that their prospect actually told them they'd provided too much information. The prospect left the meeting overwhelmed and confused. Yikes! Avoid this rookie mistake. Have confidence in the value you provide. Have a criteria you meet for the Foot in the Door and then stick to it without overdoing it. A great Foot in the Door Offer provides value and gives just enough while leaving the client wanting more.

The Foot in the Door Offer is the single most powerful addition you can make to your business — even though you make no direct profit from it the intangible benefits are invaluable. Using the Foot in the Door Offer to qualify clients, you can fill your agency's pipeline and move clients through the service offering ladder. Providing value at an enticing, low priced point means an easier decision for your prospective clients to let you impress them with your agency's talent.

Case in point. I owned my digital agency from 1999-2012 beginning at the height of the internet boom. I started small but in time had the opportunity to work with some amazing national and international brands. One of the amazing brands we worked with was Lotus Cars, an upscale specialist in the global automotive industry.

In 2008, Lotus marketing execs knocked on our door with a request for a proposal to design a microsite (which is a small, spin-off website) for a new, four-door sports car they were unveiling. We were up against several other agencies who were also pitching the microsite project. We knew we were the underdogs in this scenario since we were a small shop. As you can imagine, winning this pitch held a ton of potential for us. Thing is, when it came time to do our pitch - we decided to go a different route. We didn't pitch a microsite at all.

What we pitched instead was a discovery session where we would meet with the client to understand their goals and challenges, then develop a roadmap for what needed to be done to reach those goals and solve those challenges. They could either execute the roadmap themselves or pay someone else to do it. Hopefully, they'd choose to work with us on the execution but after the discovery there was absolutely no obligation to do so. At the time, we charged $2,500 for the discovery. When Lotus compared this to the $50K - $100K proposals they were receiving from other agencies for the microsite project, it was a no brainer for them to make a smaller commitment to my agency. With a significantly smaller investment, we were able to accelerate the decision process and speed up our sales cycle.

We clinched it by pitching the discovery up front. We did the discovery work for $2,500 and as we'd suspected, the discovery uncovered additional opportunities like social media and email marketing, and those projects naturally fell in our laps. We also did the microsite for $30,000, which was still a steal compared to what other agencies had quoted. And, after building a solid foundation with Lotus we even ended up re-designing the main Lotus Cars website for $120,000 and a monthly retainer of $5,000.

Here's the breakdown:

My Agency	Other Guys' Agencies
Discovery: $2,500	$0
Microsite: $30,000	Microsite $50,000 - $100,000
Social & Email Marketing: $60,000	$0
Main Site: $120,000	$0
Retainer for 12 months: $60,000	$0
TOTAL: $272,500	TOTAL: $50,000 - $100,000

Sure, we could have proposed marriage on that first date and possibly landed the $50,000 or $100,000 microsite project. However by starting smaller, and understanding what this prospective client needed - instead of just giving them what they *thought* they wanted - we established a relationship which led to more and higher valued work. And, even though we added more layers to the decision making process, we actually sped up the sales cycle by creating more, smaller opportunities by building trust, value, and more instances for clients to say "yes." I like to call these opportunities "milestones"... more on that later.

Lesson 3.2: Pricing to Achieve Financial Goals

Get out of your own way and stop being afraid to charge what you're worth.

Are you always feeling like you're too busy to focus on your own marketing? Too stuck in the weeds to grow something beyond it? If you're bogged down by the business that's the first sign that you aren't charging enough.

Pricing can be a really delicate matter in the agency world. A lot of agency leaders believe it's their competitive advantage. I'd argue that in most cases low balling your competition or having bargain basement pricing is actually hurting your business. You should not charge less just because you're efficient at what you do.

If I had to take an educated guess, I would say that after going through their financials, including revenue, profitability, and goals, I advise more than 90% of my one-on-one clients to increase their prices. The suggestion alone makes the hair on the back of their neck stand up. It's a scary thought... what if you end up losing pitches because your pricing is too high? Conversely I asked, what if you increase your revenue and grow your business because you're finally charging what you're worth?

BREAKING DOWN YOUR GOALS

It's a simple numbers game. In System 1 - Clarity, you should have made very specific financial goals for your agency. Start with the end in mind. Then, do some backwards math to break down your big, long term numbers into smaller, more attainable ones. Figure out what your quarterly, monthly, and weekly goals should be in order to achieve your year-end numbers.

Next, create a spreadsheet to help you forecast. List out the pricing for all the services in your Service Offering Ladder. Create formulas in the spreadsheet to determine how many clients you need to push up the ladder to achieve your quarterly, monthly, and weekly goals. If you aren't going to meet those goals and you're already too busy, it's time to increase your prices.

JUSTIFYING YOUR PRICES

While I'm a big advocate of increasing prices it obviously needs to be done strategically, with foresight and consideration. You can't just double your prices on existing clients right away. In fact, you're going to have to roll out increases with your existing clients accompanied by explanation and proof. Moving forward with new clients is a different story, however. With an understanding of your financial goals, it's likely you're going to need to charge new clients at a higher rate. This is the part that terrifies my one-on-one clients; I get it.

I often hear, *"What if we lose business because we come in too high?"* I've got a couple different responses to that questions. The first is: If you lose a pitch because your prices are too high, either they weren't your ideal client or you didn't demonstrate enough value.

Justifying your pricing is the key to landing projects with your ideal clients. Understandably, your clients want to understand why you charge what you charge. It's your duty and obligation to understand what they need and what it's worth to them, then charge accordingly. Ultimately, your justification boils down to a balance

SYSTEM 3: OFFERING

between the value you provide and what the client is willing to pay. Understanding the client's financial implications on the project can greatly impact your ability to rationalize your prices. To do that, it's important to get a handle on the answers to these questions:

- How much is the client's need/ issue costing them now?
- How much more revenue will this solution generate for your client?
- How much is a new customer worth to your client?
- What is the lifetime value of your client's customer?
- Based on answers to the above, how much is the client willing to pay to solve their issue?

But still, *"What if we lose business because we come in too high?"* My other response to this question is, *"What if you lose business because your prices aren't high enough?"*

As a matter of fact, just a couple years into owning my agency, I had a meeting set up with a company I had never heard of. In our initial conversations I gathered enough information to bring in a proposal for what (I thought) they wanted. I walked into a gorgeous, high end office space and was escorted into an amazingly impressive conference room. Shortly after, a trail of well-dressed executives marched into the conference room. Long story short, I presented them with a proposal for a $20,000 website; they didn't bat an eye at the pricing. Fingers crossed - if they worked with us, it would be our single biggest project.

I felt great about the whole pitch meeting. I didn't really get any objections on our strategy. I was pumped about it - I knew in my gut that we nailed it. Then I got the call. We didn't win the pitch. What the... ?!? The team and I went through all the emotions: puzzled, confused, upset, mad... then later, I was talking to my partner about the experience and trying to figure out what I could've done differently. That's when he asked who the client was - it was a brand I'd never heard of, Berkshire Hathaway.

Clearly, we hadn't done our homework. In 2002, worldwide Berkshire Hathaway's net worth was over $6 billion. I'm certain they were expecting to pay upward of $300,000 to $500,000 for a website. Talk about lost opportunity…. Shit.

And not only had we not done our homework on the prospect, we had undervalued ourselves. We didn't establish ourselves as an authority. We didn't demonstrate an understanding of the client's clients. We didn't know the value the client placed on having this particular issue solved. And worse, we undervalued ourselves by pricing the project much lower than expected. **We didn't land that project because we underpriced it.**

You get what you pay for. Your clients know it as well as anyone else. If you undervalue your work, your prospects will too. When you get out of your own way, you will make more money!

Lesson 3.3: Determining the Best Pricing Model

Pricing not only determines your agency's profitability but also indirectly affects every aspect of your business. Think of your business like the solar system with your prices at the center, like the sun. The planets orbiting the sun are: client retention, team retention, financial stability, and agency marketability.

I think a lot of agency leaders "figure out" pricing at the beginning, set it and forget it. However, when one element of your business has such influence on the other elements of the business, it's definitely not something to forget. Pricing must evolve just as your business does. To be effective and competitive, agency leaders should always be looking to optimize prices.

The days of structured agency fees and commission are gone. There is no longer a textbook approach to agency pricing. Your pricing model depends on your company vision, goals, and niche/specialization among other variables. There are generally three schools of thought on effective agency pricing models, each with their own list of compelling pros and cons.

#1 HOURS-BASED PRICING

There has long been a debate on whether agencies should be charging hourly. Honestly, I'm not a fan. Let me tell you why this is my absolute least favorite agency pricing model…. It's because the more efficient and effective you become at your job, the more money you lose.

Charging by the hour seems like a great option but as you get smarter and your processes become more efficient you work less on the same type of projects. When billing by the hour, your efficiency translates into fewer billable hours saving your clients money just by being better at your job!

With hourly pricing, you set a ceiling that limits your agency's potential. There are only so many hours in a day, in a week, and in a year making it difficult to scale your agency with a Hours-Based Pricing model.

For example: let's say you estimate it will take 100 hours to complete a project at $50 per hour. You'll end up making $5,000. Over time, you get more efficient at the same type of project and it only takes you 75 hours to complete the same project. If you're still charging $50 per hour, you'll bill out $3,750. That is a loss of $1,250.

Charging by the hour penalizes you for your experience, cripples your billing potential, makes your clients nervous, and encourages lower productivity. If you're pricing by the hour, you need to factor in your Fully-Burdened Rate.

Understanding and Calculating Fully-Burdened Rate

Essentially the fully-burdened rate is the all-inclusive dollar amount it costs you to do business. It includes all your operating costs, such as insurance, rent, contractors, and other overhead. The **burden rate** is the dollar amount of burden that is applied to one dollar of wages

The formula for figuring the fully-burdened rate is as follows:

$$\frac{\text{(Employee hourly wage * number of working hours per year) + other total fixed expenses}}{\text{number of actual hours worked per year}}$$

So for example, let's assume you have 3 full-time employees:

40 hours per week * 50 weeks per year = 2,000 working hours per employee
2,000 hours * 3 employees = 6,000 available working hours
$50,000 salary / 2,000 hours = $25 per hour

Let's also assume you have a fixed overhead costs of $150,000.

Your fully burdened rate would look like this:

$$\frac{(\$25 \text{ per hour} * 6{,}000 \text{ hours available}) + \$150{,}000}{5{,}000 \text{ actual hours}} = \mathbf{\$60}$$

(Note: the assumption of 5,000 actual hours is arbitrary - you'd use historical data to determine your agency's actual hours.)

Using this example, the fully-burdened rate is $60 per hour, which is just a baseline of what you should charge. So, if this agency is charging $50 per hour because they think they're covering their overhead by billing double the employee's salary rate, they'd be losing money.

#2 VALUE-BASED PRICING

Value-based pricing is the intersection between what it's worth to the client and the amount of compensation you're willing to accept. Clients hire an agency to help solve a specific issue based on the agency's unique skill set, knowledge, and experience. Value-based pricing takes all those elements into consideration and quantifies it.

Consider this analogy: A woman calls a plumber to come to her house and fix a leaky faucet. The plumber is at the woman's home for five minutes, he tightens one screw and the leak is fixed. As he makes

SYSTEM 3: OFFERING

his exit, the plumber hands the woman an invoice for $500.

Puzzled, the woman asks, "Why are you charging me $500? You were only here for five minutes."

The plumber replies, "It's $10 to tighten the screw and $490 for knowing which screw to turn."

Your knowledge, experience, and specific area of expertise is valuable to someone without the same. Unfortunately, it's really hard to get a pulse on perceived value. Effective Value Based Pricing takes time and tons of testing.

Basic Rules for Setting Up Value Pricing:

1. Gather as much information as possible from your clients so you can fully understand what they need or rather, what they think they need and how you can help. Ask a ton of questions, going beyond project logistics, in order to get a deeper understanding of the client's expectations/goals. Ask things like:

- What worries you or keeps you up at night?
- What is your business model?
- How do you make a profit?
- When was the last time you were profitable?
- What is this issue costing you in terms of revenue/profit?

2. Start with pricing that is easy to understand and explain. As business owners, we have a tendency to over complicate things like pricing. Because it makes perfect sense in our minds, we think it's crystal clear to everyone else. That's not always the case. Complex pricing can be confusing. You have to be able to explain your pricing structure to a client, so it has be something you can easily rationalize.

3. Determine client expectations and the perceived value of the project. You'll have to ask a lot of questions to get to the real meat of what they want and why. We both know there is more than one way

to get to a solution. Your client may have specific expectations and thinks there's only one way to achieve them. When you ask all the right questions and really wrap your head about the expectations you may find other routes to a solution.

4. Learn from one project to the next and test out different pricing. Test, test, test. Figure out what works and what doesn't. Then apply a combination of experience and gut instinct to get to the right pricing structure.

VALUE MODEL: Flat Rate vs. Sliding Scale Pricing

This has long been a hot topic among agencies and most certainly a question I get asked a lot. Sliding scale or flat rate for agency services? Hhhhmmm… let's see. Do you want to be viewed as an order taker or as a leading expert in your field of expertise?

When you publish a rate card you're conveying the message that your agency is an order-taker. You're staying you will do X service and it costs Y. You are basically giving your clients permission to treat you as a commodity. When you make your agency's services all about price and not about value, you are setting a precedent. And what's worse is that you cannot scale with flat-rate pricing because you're landing clients that are making their purchase decision based on price. When you try to increase your flat rates, those clients will go somewhere else cheaper because they care very little, if at all, about value.

#3 PERFORMANCE-BASED PRICING

Performance-based pricing is essentially an arrangement between buyer and seller in which the seller is paid based on the actual performance of their service. In the B2B industry, and ad agencies in particular, it can has been a sticky subject. At first glance performance-based compensation appears risky and unpredictable but there are benefits and it can be highly profitable.

SYSTEM 3: OFFERING

My friend Tom Breeze, founder and owner of Viewability, a video agency, has been operating a performance-based pricing model for years. Tom compares his business model and pricing structure to the Trojan horse story. On the outside it appears his agency takes on all the risk and fronts all the costs. In reality, they've got a killer process for qualifying their leads, they're very picky about who they'll work with, and they know how to crush it when it comes to fulfillment.

Tom's also got an undergrad degree in psychology and says the buyer goes through their own mind-game when making a decision to work with a performance-priced service provider. Performance-based pricing is received with the notion that it's a no-fail solution to the client's problem. With this mindset, the prospect basically sells themselves. They approach the engagement believing the performance-based methodology must work... because who's going to work and then not get paid for it?

Successfully educating prospects on this mentality means the agency has "pre-sold" their inbound leads on the idea of working this way. There's very little objection handling or hard selling necessary because the prospect already buys into the process, value, and benefits.

Performance-based pricing also has an element of "float" to it, meaning the revenue from current clients funds the activity for future clients. However, within a couple months they're self-sustaining.

It takes a shift in mindset. A results-driven agency is dedicated to only taking on clients with a greater lifetime value. The drawbacks, of course, are the upfront cost and the lack of predictability that long term, project or retainer clients provide. However, a highly effective specialists in a narrow niche will find the benefits outweigh the disadvantages.

Basic Rules for Setting Up Performance Pricing:

1. Do not act as an agent, act as an affiliate. Rather than structuring

client relationships like most service-based businesses, you should establish an agency-client relationship. Success means creating a foundation where the agency works *with* their clients instead of *for* them because the final outcome has financial implications on both parties.

2. Know the formula for what makes a good client. Keep a list of specific questions and criteria that determines who you will and will not work with; also go for quality over quantity of clients. Fewer clients means more time to spend on guaranteeing successful results.

3. Work directly with the decision-maker. This is actually pretty important for all agency pricing models. Make sure you always deal with the person who has full accountability for determining success and for seeing to it that you get paid.

4. Maintain realistic expectations when using this pricing model. Goals need to be measurable and attainable. Ask your clients these questions and get answers before engaging in a transaction: Do they know their current cost per lead? (If not, that's a major red flag.) What would they like it to be? Is it an evergreen offer that just needs more promotion? Has the funnel already been tested?

SYSTEM 3: OFFERING

Recap: System 3 - Offering

This system is all about structuring your agency's offering and pricing it accurately. (Hint: you're probably not charging enough. I'll show you why!) Getting this part right will have an immediate and lasting impact on your business.

▶ **Lesson 3.1: Creating a Service Offering Ladder**

Naturally you want to land projects that are right in your agency's sweet spot and the bigger, the better. But pitching your core service at the first meeting is like proposing marriage on the first date. Instead, create a service offering ladder and have clients stairstep their way to increasingly larger projects:

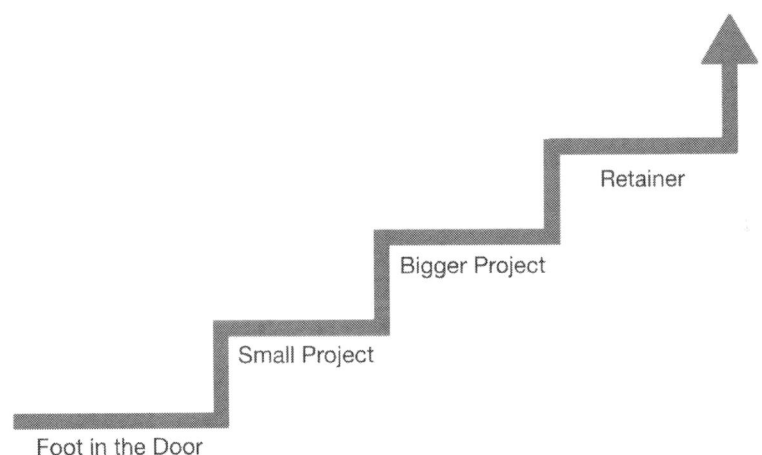

The best way to initiate a new client relationship is with the Foot in the Door Offer. This is a low cost, high value service that establishes trust and authority. A Foot in the Door is an easy decision for the client to make, yet not a money maker for your agency. Following a positive experience with the Foot in the Door, clients are 20X more likely to do business with your agency again.

ACCELERATING YOUR AGENCY

▶ Lesson 3.2: Pricing to Achieve Financial Goals

The vast majority of agencies I work with aren't charging enough. And usually, they know they're worth it but they fear the fallout from implementing an increase. Start charging what you're worth! Break down your financial goals into quarterly, monthly, and weekly goals then set your prices accordingly.

Set your fears to rest… if you lose business because your prices are too high then you weren't speaking to the right prospect. Create a better qualification process so you don't waste time on prospects who can't afford you.

Your prospects know the old adage, "you get what you pay for." If you undercharge you're setting an expectation for mediocrity. Charge what you're worth and justify it by producing your clients' desired results.

▶ Lesson 3.3: Determining the Best Pricing Model

There are 3 common ways to price your agency services:

1. Hours Pricing

I'm not a fan. As you get more efficient and produce better work in less time you lose money. If you're pricing by the hour, you need to factor in your Fully-Burdened Rate. The formula for figuring the fully-burdened rate is as follows:

$$\frac{(\text{Employee hourly wage} * \text{number of working hours per year}) + \text{other total fixed expenses}}{\text{number of actual hours worked per year}}$$

2. Value-Based Pricing

This is the fine balance between fair market value and what you deem acceptable compensation. The key is to gather as much information as possible to fully understand the scope of the work and the desired

SYSTEM 3: OFFERING

result. Keep pricing easy to explain therefore easily understood. Be clear about expectations, and monitor and report on results in order to demonstrate value.

3. Performance-Based Pricing

Pricing based on performance is the least common pricing model but, with the right processes in place, can be highly profitable. Performance-based pricing is essentially an arrangement between buyer and seller in which the seller is paid based on the actual performance of their service. Often prospects are "pre-sold" to businesses that operate under this pricing model.

Get more tools, instructional videos, and agency document templates at TheAgencyPlaybook.com

SYSTEM 4

Prospecting

ACCELERATING YOUR AGENCY

With equal importance placed on three channels of procuring prospects, your odds of success are three times greater.

If you rely heavily on word-of-mouth referrals or have a very limited approach to prospecting you'll learn a ton in this section. It's all about the multi-channel approach a successful agency needs in order to capture leads, keep their pipeline full of prospects, and convert more leads into opportunities. I always suggest having a three-pronged approach to prospecting so you're not too reliant on just one form of cultivating new business.

Too many agencies rely on one channel for generating leads. In order to maximize your potential for success, your lead generation activity should have equal emphasis in the areas of inbound, outbound, and strategic partnerships.

In this chapter, you'll learn:

1. About your low-hanging fruit and how it can bring immediate revenue.
2. Outbound strategies that will get the initial meeting with your ideal clients.
3. Inbound strategies beyond blogging and the occasional social post.
4. What content your ideal clients are looking for and how you can deliver it.
5. What strategic partnerships you should be developing.
6. How to find/build a community where your ideal clients convene.
7. The best way to capture leads instead of just generating them.

Lesson 4.1: Low-Hanging Fruit

Most people believe prospecting means finding *new* clients and creating *new* opportunities. However we often neglect the "old"

SYSTEM 4: PROSPECTING

opportunities that, for whatever reason, didn't quite pan out. Low-hanging fruit is a metaphor for the opportunities that are closest and within easy reach. In sales, your low-hanging fruit is the ripest and ready for picking. These "fruits" are past clients or potential clients who are already aware of your agency services and may just need a nudge toward making a purchase decision or a reminder that you are the advisor who can guide them to a solution for their problem.

This lesson is an exercise on identifying your low-hanging fruit and reconnecting with them. There are two categories of prospects you'll need to consider: (1) past clients who haven't worked with you in a while and (2) lost opportunities with those who've never worked with you. You should create a spreadsheet with tabs for both categories then fill in the spreadsheet and use it as your call list.

PAST CLIENTS

Obviously, these are clients your agency has worked with previously. They're aware of your level of awesome but have not engaged in another project, whether it be due to timing, budget, or reasons unknown. It's time to re-knock on their door. To create a call list, use these column headers in your spreadsheet:

- Who you worked with, including contact information and title.
- What project or service your agency performed for them.
- Any significant successes or learning that resulted from your work.
- The date of last contact with this client.
- Any relevant new strategies or next steps that could be executed for greater results.

NEW PROSPECTS

These are prospective clients you've never worked with but are already aware of what your agency does. (And perhaps with your newly crafted Elevator Pitch it will be even clearer to them.) Consider people involved in past pitches you lost, prospects who didn't have the budget, as well as people in your social network, such as LinkedIn. Create a spreadsheet with column headers such as:

- Who you've spoken with, including contact information and title.
- What problems or issues are they having?
- What objections or obstacles have prevented them from working with you in the past?
- What does success look like for them?
- What is the consequence if the problem or issues are not solved?
- How can you guide them toward their solution?

(If any of this rings a bell, *good!* This is the very same framework we used for establishing your Positioning Script. When you're reaching out to new prospects, use the same strategy.)

Next it's time to set aside time to make the calls. And I do mean actual, old school **phone calls** - no emails. Your low-hanging fruit has the greatest potential for turning into real business but only if you nurture the relationship right from the start. So, if you must leave a voicemail be really specific about who you are and why you're calling. **Do not** leave a voicemail that says you're "just calling to check in." We both know no one returns those types of calls.

Instead, leave a voicemail giving them just enough information to make them want to return your call. Say something like: *"Hi Joe, last time we talked you were having a really hard time with X. I know you would love to Y and I have had some great success doing Z with other clients. This is a new strategy that you have to try. I'd love to chat about it so call me back. If I don't hear from you today, I'll try calling you again tomorrow."*

Then you have to actually follow-through and make the call again the next day. When your prospect realizes you've got something innovative to share and you're reliable (by calling when you say you will) he will make time to listen.

Your low-hanging fruit should be an easy sell because they're already interested and educated. Pursuing low-hanging fruit is a great way to bring in some immediate revenue while you're planting seeds for a new crop of prospects. Be certain to notate your progress and continue to develop your low-hanging fruit spreadsheet by updating and adding to it regularly. Set a reminder on your calendar to make low-hanging fruit calls every quarter.

Lesson 4.2: Outbound Strategies

Cold calling is tough, no doubt about it. In this section, you'll learn several outbound sales strategies that can help you book new business meetings and open your agency up to new opportunities.

The best way to get your foot in the door is by doing detailed research on the business you're targeting and discovering how you can help them in a unique way. Using your Positioning Script and unique selling proposition, you can turn a cold call into a real conversation. The goal is to demonstrate your authority in a specific area while presenting a new and innovative business growth idea.

WHAT CLIENTS WANT

I had the opportunity to talk to Del Ross, the former VP of Sales & Marketing at InterContinental Hotel Group (IHG). Del was a guest on my podcast and gave some great insider's insight into what big brands love and hate about cold calls from agencies.

Del said he would get at least one cold call per day, and many more cold emails per day. The only ones that managed to grab attention were the ones who had an expertise or specialization in a specific area. He automatically dismissed any agency who claimed they could "do everything" (ie. jack-of-all-trades but master of none). Del was never shopping for "everything" so he never wanted an agency who could do "everything." However, at various times he had needs for certain, specific things and that's why specialty agencies beat out generalists every time.

What really got Del's attention was when an agency would call him and propose an innovative solution or idea that could help accomplish a specific goal. Remember the Alfred/Batman analogy? Del was looking for new ways to achieve results and needed a trusted advisor to help him get there. His marketing budget at IHG included some discretionary funds and Del could spend up to $50,000 just testing one new idea. So if he was presented with an interesting strategy backed by information and data, he'd lean into it.

Education and assertiveness are key in getting a client's attention. An agency with a point of view or belief based on data and proven results is worth a listen. Clients want an agency to be their advisor and tell them 'X' activity would lead to 'Y' results and 'Z' is the plan to orchestrate it.

On the other hand, too much assertiveness or uneducated claims were a total turnoff for Del. He absolutely hated getting calls by agencies claiming they can do it better. He says agencies should never make claims to do something better than the current agency. You never know what's going on behind the scenes and presumptuous claims are a real turn off. Don't throw someone else under the bus in order to get ahead. Instead find a way to put your agency in the spotlight by offering something *different* - not necessarily better, just something better than status quo.

Straight from the source, here are some other pet peeves...

- A cold call that starts out asking for 20-minutes of their time to "see how they can help." Clients don't have 20-minutes of extra time for you to tell them how they can spend money with you.
- Self-serving calls are a major turnoff. This means cold calling a client and pushing your service because it's what you want to sell, with no regard as to what the client actually needs.
- Agencies who just want to help a client spend your budget instead of taking the time to first understand their goals.

SYSTEM 4: PROSPECTING

- A cold call that includes rattling off the agency's achievements, awards, and list of other clients. (Hint: nothing you-related in the first conversation.)

The key takeaway from my interview with Del was to concentrate on the prospect's goals and introduce something new that will knock their socks off. You will land a first meeting if you can demonstrate your expertise in the field and back up your claims with data and proof.

COLD CALLING STRATEGIES

First, start by making a list of 50-100 ideal clients. Then depending on your agency's structure, the lead sales team member (and sometimes that's the owner, who also wears a dozen other hats) should have a goal to make 10+ calls per day.

Next, research all the brands on your list. Find out the decision maker and don't spin your wheels talking to anyone except that person. Do your homework on the organization, not just topline information but really zero in on specifics. I recommend one or a mix of both these cold calling strategies to get a first appointment booked:

1. Audit Strategy

You can use technology, data, and other tools to identify something they're doing, or not doing. Use this information to show them a better or different approach. My agency, for example collected information on our prospects' Google Adwords spending. We coupled that information with research showing that every dollar spent beyond a certain cap was wasted. We offered an audit to show our prospects where they were losing money. Leading off a sales call with this information is super helpful and informative.

2. Education Strategy

In this type of call, you'll use your knowledge of your prospect's struggles and goals to your advantage. Consider the Positioning

Script exercise - what challenges do they face? What does success look like for them? What is the tragic result if they don't take action? Create a workshop or lunch and learn event that focuses on solving your prospects pain point. You can use your cold call as a verbal invitation to a live event where you further educate your prospects.

Another way to educate prospects is to share competitive information. You can do a competitive analysis and share their competitor's strategy with them. Point out what the competition is doing that they're not doing and how you can help engineer a solution for them.

Find the angle that works best for you and give it a try. Craft a message using one of the strategies above or some hybrid of them. Cold calling can be especially tough if you feel like you don't know enough about the prospect's organization in order to convey a relevant message. So, if you consistently sell to the same decision makers it's OK to make some assumptions. Assume that they have similar objectives and face similar challenges as your existing clients. For example, most marketers today are under intense pressure to bring in more high quality leads or to justify their marketing spend.

If you typically sell to certain industries, immerse yourself in them. Join their associations, attend their meetings, get their newsletters, and dig into their websites. Another great resource for learning more is via LinkedIn and Facebook groups. These are both great places to learn the lingo and gain an understanding of particular industry jargon.

Lesson 4.3: Inbound Strategies

Putting the right content in the right place, at the right time makes you relevant and helpful.

The next piece to the prospecting puzzle is a phenomenal inbound marketing strategy. Of course the goal of inbound is to bring

SYSTEM 4: PROSPECTING

potential customers to you, rather than fighting for them in other ways.

The way to master inbound marketing is to do more with less. Most people think inbound = blog posts. That's true but it doesn't stop there. In this section, I'll walk you through creating helpful content your prospects want and need, plus how you can use it, repurpose it and slice it into micro content to give it legs.

CONTENT CREATION

Building more on the Positioning Script exercise from System 2, consider your ideal clients' challenges, issues, needs, and desires. Your content must be a means to an end on one of these items. It must be searchable and cause your prospects to pause long enough to check you out.

As you continue to learn more about your leads, you can really personalize your messages to their specific needs. Until the ideas really start flowing, find out where your prospects congregate and pay attention to their chatter. Find them on LinkedIn or Facebook groups. Find out what other industry-specific communities they're gathering in. Join those groups and be a fly on the wall to observe activity. Read through the members' posts and comments. Note which posts get the most feedback or comment threads - those are hot topics! Find some common themes and start generating content ideas that center around delivering helpful answers to those issues. Evolve from being a fly on the wall to being a servant to that community.

As you create a list of content topic ideas, don't be afraid to be really specific with your content ideas. Drill down the exact topics that are relevant to your very specific niche and specialization. Be sure to use their language - talk their their talk in order to be perceived as an authority.

One of the real gurus on content marketing is Jay Baer. Jay is a business strategist, speaker, writer, podcast show host, and founder of Convince & Convert, a social media and content marketing consultancy. Jay has consulted with more than 700 companies including some huge ones like Nike, Allstate, Petco, and Columbia Sportswear.

He says the best way to grow your business is to create content that is useful. So useful, in fact, that people would actually want to pay for it but they don't have to because you're giving it away for free. This type of super helpful, free content will help you break through the noise and be heard above everyone else. And yes, you can give away all your best stuff for free without sabotaging your business.

Jay tells his client not to get hung up on "giving away too much" because there's no such thing as a secret ingredient anymore. You don't have to have a proprietary lockdown on your business strategy. What you have is the same plan as the next agency and the client's decision will come down to trust and authority. Strong content will build both.

Giving it away for free doesn't mean you'll lose business. People just want to know the recipe to the so-called "secret sauce." In the end, they still want to hire someone else to do all the work. The real secret to great content marketing is to take everything you know and give it away one nugget at a time.

BEYOND BLOGGING

You probably already have a blog but you get extra credit if you are using video or other rich media. If you aren't using video or a media form that interacts with your prospects, you're losing out. Check it out - numbers don't lie:

- Adding a video to your website can increase the chance of a front page Google result by up to 53x.
- Using videos in email marketing has been shown to double click-through rates.

SYSTEM 4: PROSPECTING

- 71% of marketers say that video conversion rates consistently outperform other marketing content.
- Audiences are 10x more likely to engage with video content than text-only blogs or social posts.

These numbers make a pretty compelling case for use of video in your marketing. But there's some psychological benefits, too. As a society, we live in a very technological era. We've spent the better part of a decade on social media. Status updates and Tweets are the norm. But as humans we crave more personal contact. When we consume content in video form we find it more personal. And when it's a live feed, it's all that more authentic, raw, and real.

Video is *critical* to helping people connect with, remember, and care about your agency. Consider these statistics:

- Videos tend to be perceived as stories, and stories are **22x** more memorable than facts alone.
- Positive emotions created by watching a video can actually impact your viewers' buying decisions.
- The human brain processes visuals **60,000x** faster than text.

Simply put, video and rich media can tap into your prospect's psyche and emotions in a way that plain text or static images cannot. Using video doesn't have to mean high production quality. Use your phone when the mood strikes you and answer a question or talk about a topic. Record yourself (most people don't really love that part, but you get used to it) and post it raw and unedited.

Edited, production-quality videos have their time and place but people also like to see uncut, real footage. Hop on Facebook Live, Instagram Stories, Snapchat, or whatever other social media applications your prospects are using and just start doing it.

PODCASTING

I'm a huuuuuge fan of podcasting. I can't say enough about what it's done for my business, personally. And yes, you too can host a podcast. It's so much easier than you think. You don't need to have a fancy airwave-quality voice; it's for everyone. Very few people are actually doing it but I'm telling you what, people are listening and they're looking for the content you want to offer. There are a ton of benefits to using podcasting as an inbound marketing strategy:

First of all, the podcasting space is less crowded. Stats vary but there's something like 5 million+ active blogs and only 500,000 active podcasts. Those are great odds! Podcasting is far less cluttered so you can find and reach your target audience.

Podcasts live forever. So, there's potential for exponential growth as new prospects listen to old episodes. Times change but in most industries the challenges and issues stay the same. Podcast content is evergreen, and evergreen content is the most efficient inbound marketing.

Also, people are still discovering podcasts. Listenership is growing and by starting a podcast sooner rather than later you'll get in on the ground level. Listeners are downloading podcasts to listen to on the go: during their commute, working out, waiting in long lines, etc. When they find something they love, they're even binge-listening! The challenge is being patient while you build an audience. Podcasting isn't something that grows overnight. It can take six to twelve months to grow your audience. You can accelerate this by sharing your podcasts on social media and asking your guests to do the same, but truly it's something that grows organically. If patience is a virtue, be top-notch virtuous when it comes to building a listenership.

When you host a podcast you'll gain credibility and establish authority with your audience. As you continue to provide helpful content and value, you'll earn guest interviews with experts, adding more impact to your credibility.

Starting a Podcast

I had the great honor of interviewing Pat Flynn on my podcast. If you don't know about Pat, you should immediately put this book down and go check him out. Pat is the successful guy behind Smart Passive Income – a major resource for entrepreneurs looking to scale their business. He's also *the guru* in the world of podcasting. I credit Pat's podcast course for my success podcasting over the past three years.

Maybe you've been thinking of starting a podcast but you've got some hang ups about it. You're not alone. There are several common fears a lot of people face which hold them back from getting started. Pat gave some advice on getting over those fears and embracing this killer inbound opportunity:

"What if people can't find it?"

They will find it as long as you're specific in who you're targeting. People search for podcasts based on their interests, problems, and focus. If you're searchable in one of those areas, they will find your podcast. It just takes a little time to build your audience so be patient and let it grow.

"What if I can't come up with show content?"

There are a couple different formats you can try out and see what sticks.

Invite expert guests on your show to be interviewed on a specific topic that interests your audience. People like authors, prospects, existing customers, and forum owners make great guests. Interviews are a win-win because you get some great show content and the guest gets to promote their business, book, forum, or area expertise.

Another popular show format is Q&A, like my #AskSwenk Show. Take common questions and record your answers, solution, or advice. This is an awesome way to establish authority and credibility with your target audience.

"What if people don't like it?"

The key is to help your audience. Choose topics that are relevant and helpful to them. Don't guess what people want to know – research it online. Find out where your audience congregates online and see what problems, issues, or questions they are posting. Develop your show topics surrounding those issues and helping solve those problems. Don't sell right away, just help.

"How can I find my 'hosting' voice?"

Everyone feels the same way and you'll get over it in time. Pat says finding your voice is just trial and error. You'll get into a groove but in order for that to happen you have to start somewhere. Go back and listen to yourself, critique yourself, and do better next time. Also, read the comments that follow your podcasts and make changes based on that feedback.

The best thing you can do is: be you. It's ok to look at other successful podcasters and model after them, but don't copy their style. Be authentic and your "hosting voice" will develop by itself.

"I don't understand the technology and equipment."

Pat says the technology has come a long way since he started in 2010. You just have to research and education yourself.

The thing about fear of something like this is that it's a sign you're about to do something that could be a real game changer. So embrace the fear and psych yourself up for extreme awesomeness.

You absolutely have to specialize. Pick a niche and be super specific on who you're helping. When you try to serve everyone, you end up serving no one. The more specific the better. In fact, when you upload your podcast to iTunes, Stitcher, etc. you need to select a specific category in order to be searchable.

Also, be prepared to be super patient. In Pat's experience he says it takes a year or two to build a following and see real results. He stresses patience when you are trying to build a community of followers. If you're putting yourself out there, word will spread - but it doesn't happen overnight.

MULTI-CHANNEL DISTRIBUTION

Multi-channel distribution is the most efficient way to circulate your content. You absolutely need to get your helpful content (whether it's video, podcast, or plain old blog) out in all the places where your ideal clients are hanging out. And if you want to be on your agency blog, plus Facebook, Twitter, Instagram, and YouTube (and who knows what else might exist in the future?!) it can overwhelming. But, it doesn't have to be. There's no reason to reinvent the wheel in order to be present among various media outlets.

I'm a big fan of doing more with less.

The trick is to create one piece of mega-awesome macro content and then slice it into bite-sized content you can use elsewhere. We follow this same principle with my #AskSwenk Q&A show. It's been brilliant in terms of doing more with less. It gives my content legs and involves so much less work than would appear.

First, we record the #AskSwenk video of me answering two or three questions. Most videos end up being three or four minutes long. We edit those down into shorter, stand alone videos with one question each. That means we shot one video and turned it into four individual pieces of content. (One longer video trimmed into an additional three shorter videos for a total of four.) We write a summary of the questions/answers and post those on the blog. We capture still images and standalone quotes from the video to create images that we can post on social media. The videos get uploaded to YouTube and iTunes, as well.

ACCELERATING YOUR AGENCY

I know, it seems complicated, but it's not. It's actually pretty quick and seamless. Here's the workflow every piece of content goes through:

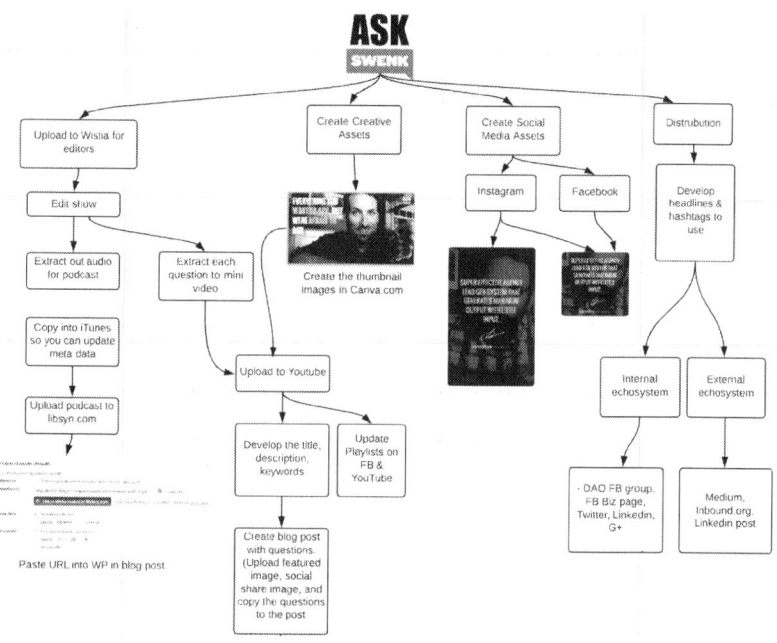

SYSTEM 4: PROSPECTING

It looks like this takes a ton of time but I swear it doesn't. Like I said, I'm a big fan of having the right systems in place. I outsource the editing and my team uses some great technology to manage all our social posts. Do more with less by having the right systems in place.

Lesson 4.4: Strategic Partnerships

Using strategic partners as your third method of prospecting can be highly effective when implemented with careful thought and purpose. Both parties can benefit significantly by building an alliance within the same niche. I would add the caveat that strategic partnerships does not translate to *"referral network."* Referrals are great but they aren't scalable. Strategic partners build a relationship of mutual respect and trust with the intentions of helping each other grow their businesses through endorsements and goodwill.

If you don't already have an alliance with a couple strategic partners, start by making a list of companies that are going after the same niche as your agency. Consider businesses of all shapes and sizes; think outside the box. You could even add other agencies to your list. (Yes, really!) Think about other agencies who are going after the same target as you and who offer complementary services to yours. I'll reiterate this isn't a handshake agreement to send each other business. It's bigger than just referrals - it's a growth strategy for both of you.

This is more than a transactional relationship so you'll also want to make sure you're looking at partners with a matched vision and culture. So look for companies that can bring you a pool of clients or strengthen your credibility, among other things. As in any partnership, it's in everyone's best interest to be certain you think, work, and feel similarly because you'll work together closely for an extended period of time.

Making your list should take no more than an hour and could include a dozen or more business names. With a good working list of partners, list out the potential benefits each party will receive by working in partnership. Specifically identify areas where you can offer great benefit to a potential partner by aligning with their goals. (Of course you'll benefit too, but we're looking first at ways to make this an attractive offer to your potential partners.)

When you're ready to start making a connection with a strategic partner make sure you are positioning the relationship properly. I like to say, make a deposit before you make a withdrawal. Meaning, do something *for someone* before asking them to do something for you. You'll get better traction with your strategic partners if you establish goodwill right off the bat.

Start slow and learn how to manage one partnership at a time. Learn as you go and you'll know when the time is right to consider taking on an additional strategic partner.

Lesson 4.5: Building a Community

Your agency is working in a specific niche and you have a well-defined target market. So, why not connect these like-minded people? The best way to achieve a connection for them is by building a community where they can collaborate, idea-share and help one another. I use the communities I have created for building content, building trust, and…. of course, building sales.

In the Content Creation lesson, you spent time trolling through the existing online communities where your ideal clients congregate. The ancillary benefit to that exercise is learning the importance of these communities. Your ideal clients are seeking out the advice of their peers. They're talking to one another, sharing experiences, asking questions, even showing vulnerability by exposing their own problems publicly. Why is this? Because in an era of digi-techi-virtual-everything, people still want to feel connected. They want to feel like they belong to something. They want to know there's a human on the other end of the keyboard. So, as a means to that end, I suggest creating your own online community in Facebook,

LinkedIn, or elsewhere. Community creation is a fantastic method for pooling together new prospects. Just be certain any personal gain on your part is secondary to meeting the needs of the community members.

Chris Brogan, community building expert, says we should consider these **3 Golden Rules** for building a successful community.

1. Business is about belonging. Remember the goal of the forum is for collaborating and idea sharing. It's not a new vehicle for your self-promotion. You can be a contributor to the community by posting helpful content. However more frequently than that, you should make members feel understood, heard, and appreciated. I suggest a 1:3(+) ratio in promoted posts/comments. That means one self-serving post to every three or more answers to members questions. Don't be that guy (or gal). Your social community will certainly lose members quickly if you only fill the newsfeed with a bunch of promotional material.

Along these same lines, define who is and is not allowed to be part of your online community. Restrict it to your niche or specialization. Make it a closed or private group to maintain control. I started a Facebook community for digital agency owners. We only allow digital agency owners into the group. If someone requests access and their job title is not immediately recognizable as an Agency Owner or principle, we deny access to the group. We want members to feel they belong and are among people in their same boat.

2. Access is the new aloofness. Be available and reach out personally. People buy from people, not from brands or businesses. It's OK to have someone else manage the community but be present and available by actively posting, commenting, and answering questions yourself. Most common social media applications have a private message function. Use that to reach out to people personally but only when you see a need or an avenue in which you can help them navigate toward a solution - never for a sales pitch.

3. Connect and serve. Community engagement goes a long way. If you can connect people to each other and provide value for both, your extension of goodwill will gain their loyalty and trust. Encourage and support the exchange of knowledge among members. Be a servant to the community; help especially when you have nothing to gain.

The role of the group administrators is to be both an ambassador for the group as well as policing content and screening members. Members should fit your carefully defined criteria and be true to the intention of the group. Delete posts and block users who aren't. It's not about the quantity of community members, it's about the quality. And remember, just because you created and manage the community, it doesn't belong to you - it belongs to its members. Above all else, keep true to the needs and challenges of your community members.

Lesson 4.6: The ABC's of Marketing Automation

It's important and necessary to have a system for keeping your leads engaged after your initial contact. Having automated marketing in place has allowed me to build trust and convert more leads into opportunities and sales for my current business, JasonSwenk.com. And damn do I wish I had this in place when I owned my agency!

Don't confuse automated marketing with some BS system that pushes your latest blog post out to everyone on your list. The secret to effective automated marketing is what I call Milestone Marketing. This is the marketing automation framework I developed which evolves with the decisions my prospects make every time I reach out to them. The fundamental philosophy is breaking your automated campaigns into simple milestones that behave dynamically different based on the user's engagement.

It's starts by knowing who, where, what and when to capture your leads. I use an ABC formula for **A**ttract, **B**uild, and **C**onvert.

A - ATTRACT

Attract traffic to your agency website. In Lesson 2.4 you gave your agency's website a major makeover. Next, a newly redeveloped inbound strategies should be providing organic traffic. You are probably (or should be) attracting some paid traffic to your site as well.

B - BUILD

Build leads. The most effective way of building leads is by using a lead magnet, which is a moral bribe for something of value in exchange for a prospect's email address or phone number.

Keys to an effective lead magnet:

1. Be super-specific on who it's for in order to increase your conversion rate. (Trust me, it won't scare off the right clients.)
2. Offer immediate gratification, be true to your word, and deliver immediately.
3. Have a perceived value that is greater than the pain of a prospect providing their contact info (phone or email).
4. Promise one big thing or one major payoff, as opposed to promising a bunch of little things.
5. Speak to the known desired end result.
6. Condense to be consumable in under six minutes and be engaging.
7. Provide an actual high value, or an "ah-ha moment" as a take away.

Taking all this into consideration, think about what you can offer that would be of value without giving away the farm. Maybe it's a worksheet, cheat sheet, or template that improves your leads' business. Maybe it's a list of 5 - 7 best practices or how-to's that solve a problem for them. Other great ideas include survey results, webinars, case studies, video training.... anything goes as long as it meets the criteria. Do not be salesy - there should not be any strings attached to this offer, other than an email address.

Consider what your prospects need or want; what problem do they have that you can solve? Don't think big. Think small. Remember: super specific. Brainstorm your lead magnet offer by answering these questions:

- Who is it for?
- What are the benefits?
- What need does this meet?
- What are some sub-benefits?
- What will they get, what is the outcome?
- What is the consequence if they don't accept your offer?

Opting in through a lead magnet is your prospect's way of raising his or her hand, indicating interest, and giving you the green light to send marketing in their direction.

C- CONVERT

Convert leads into opportunities or sales. Marketing automation using my Milestone Marketing framework will help you convert a greater percentage of prospects into clients.

MILESTONE MARKETING

A few years ago, I started experimenting with my automated marketing, and guess what I discovered? Not everyone is ready to buy what I'm selling! I began giving them options to meet them where they're at... not ready to buy? That's OK! Everyone is at a different stage in their decision making journey. So, Milestone Marketing is a method of breaking down marketing campaigns into Milestones that evolve based on users engagement and interaction.

As a marketer implementing Milestone Marketing campaigns, your goal is to identify the tiny moments that ultimately lead your prospects to the desired outcome. For those who don't follow the path to your desired outcome, Milestone Marketing campaigns are bolted together to address hesitation (for whatever reason), decrease lost opportunities and increase your conversions.

The 3 B's of Milestone Marketing:

1. **Break** campaigns into smaller goals known as "milestones".
2. **Build-in** contingencies in order to handle objections and overcome obstacles.
3. **Bolt together** campaigns to lose fewer opportunities.

Milestone Marketing is all about the baby steps or mini-funnels which allow for contingencies and lets you bolt one campaign to another for complementary or related products/services. Milestone Marketing takes many variables into consideration and changes the course of the path based on the prospect's level of interaction with the campaign, all on autopilot using your marketing automation tool.

A few key points, disclaimers, and caveats to this section:
- I do not recommend or endorse any particular systems, tools, or software. I do, of course, have my favorites but those may change as technology develops so I've chosen not to list anything particular here. I do consistently update the list on my website, JasonSwenk.com/tools, if you are looking for my recommendations on the latest and greatest.
- When planning your automated emails, it's important to time them to be sent when your recipient is most likely to respond and engage. To achieve this, you'll need software that can send emails in a 24 hour interval from the time of first interaction (for example, it sends a follow-up email timed 24 hours from the the time the initial email is read). In other words, you should not blast mass emails to your entire list at once but rather use software to "fish while the fish are biting."
- I rely heavily on video content and put a lot of credence in its value. I've found it to be the vehicle which receives the most

interaction from my prospects and clients, so I use it in most of my automated marketing campaigns. Because of this, I have software which tells me whether a video has been viewed or not, whether it's been seen in its entirety and if not, at what point it was stopped. I am able to qualify the prospect and move them onto the next Milestone (or not) based on the amount of video content viewed. This information has been incredibly valuable. If you wind up using videos, I highly recommend using a tool with the same functionality.

- I never have my leads go through the same campaign twice. You should definitely bolt campaigns together and you certainly want to try different angles to make a sale. However, you don't want to be redundant because that will lead to being viewed as irrelevant or even lazy.

- When determining milestones, think about all the various ways a user might engage with your marketing. They could open a PDF, they could watch an embedded video, they could reply with one word or phrase, they could text you… The possibilities are endless. Don't let the lack of technology scare you off. If you can think of it, I promise someone else has too, and they've developed the technology for it as well.

- Stay on top of your tech game. Don't just assume that what you're using is the best available. Technology evolves and you'll need to be flexible in allowing your campaigns and strategies to evolve with technological advances. Tweaking is not only OK, it is vital.

Recap: System 4 - Prospecting

I always advise a three-pronged approach to prospecting so you're not too reliant on any one form of cultivating new business. These three avenues of sales prospecting are: inbound, outbound, and strategic partnerships.

▶ **Lesson 4.1: Low-Hanging Fruit**

Low-hanging fruit are either (1) past clients who haven't worked with you in a while and (2) lost opportunities with those who've never worked with you. You can create a spreadsheet with tabs for both categories and fill in the spreadsheet and use it as your call list. This is just one part, perhaps the easiest part, of an outbound strategy because these are not cold calls.

▶ **Lesson 4.2: Outbound Strategies**

Outbound sales can be super tough but when you do research and make pitch calls with a purpose the results are much more successful. Two strategies can help with outbound sales calls:

1. Audit Strategy - the Sales Rep presents specific information on in an area where the prospective client needs improvement. This type of call is fact and data driven.
2. Education Strategy - helps the prospect learn a way to solve a particular challenge or pain point in his business. Typically this is done in workshop or presentation style setting and provides significant learning and valuable information.

▶ **Lesson 4.3: Inbound Strategies**

You'll have greater success with an inbound strategy that involves providing value and helping not selling. Inbound efforts must go beyond blogging and have to include rich media, such as video, which makes prospects 10X more likely to engage. Podcasting can be another amazing form inbound marketing. It give you the

ACCELERATING YOUR AGENCY

opportunity to reach your target audience when they're searching for information so you can gain credibility and authority.

▶ Lesson 4.4: Strategic Partnerships

Strategic partners build a relationship with the intention of each partner helping the other grow through endorsements and goodwill. Perfect partners are other businesses who target the same market as your agency and/or have complimentary services. These partnerships differ from referrals. Referrals are intermittent, unreliable, and not at all scalable.

▶ Lesson 4.5: Building a Community

Do some research to see what types of online forums and communities exist for your target audience. Chance are there isn't much out there in terms of places they can collaborate, idea-share, and help one another. You can build a community using LinkedIn, Facebook, or other social networks. The three rules for building a community:

1. Business is about belonging. Make community members feel welcomed and appreciated. Don't use the forum for spewing promotional posts.
2. Access is the new aloofness. Make yourself available and be helpful without being pushy. Comment on posts and direct message when appropriate in order to help community members navigate towards a solution.
3. Connect and serve. Extend goodwill by making recommendations and connect members to one another. Encourage, support, and provide value. Act as if you have nothing to gain and you will gain everything in return.

▶ Lesson 4.6: The ABC's of Marketing Automation

Effective marketing automation uses an ABC formula:

A - Attract traffic to your agency website.

B - Build your list.
C - Convert leads into sales.

A lead magnet is the most effective way to build your list. A lead magnet is a moral bribe for information in exchange for a prospect's email address of phone number. Lead magnets are super specific nuggets of valuable information which solve a problem and have a perceived value that is greater than the pain of giving up contact information.

You can increase your conversion rate by building Milestone Marketing into your automated marketing campaigns. These "milestones" are mini-funnels and change based on the recipient's engagement with your marketing.

Get more tools, instructional videos, and agency document templates at TheAgencyPlaybook.com

SYSTEM 5

5 Sales

ACCELERATING YOUR AGENCY

Once you've positioned yourself properly as "the choice" and establish an effective multi-channel approach to prospecting, the next natural step in growing your agency is perfecting your sales with proven strategies and tactics. I like to walk my one-on-one clients through a couple very distinct strategies we used at my agency in order to close more business. As we grew and worked our way up the food chain these same tactics helped us move from smaller, local clients to larger, national brands like Hitachi, AT&T, and Lotus Cars.

In this chapter, you'll learn:
1. Strategies for qualifying prospects so you work with just the right ones.
2. The stages of sales and what they mean in terms of conversion rates.
3. All the important sections of a proposal and the order in which they should appear.
4. A strategy for getting inside the prospect's head.
5. Tactics for handling sales objections.
6. How to build, manage, and compensate a sales team.

Lesson 5.1: Qualifying Prospects

Qualifying your prospects means more than just making sure they're able to pay you. If you've ever spent time spinning your wheels on a pitch only to find out you weren't talking to the decision maker, they don't have the right budget, or they have an unrealistic expectations, you aren't alone. It's a common mistake tons of agencies make. It's because they never took the time to make sure the expectations of both parties are aligned.

N.B.A.T. = NEED, BUDGET, TIMING, AUTHORITY

When an agency is young and hungry to do the work they love (or perhaps cashflow is tight and they NEED the work), they don't ask enough questions and end up taking on projects that aren't the right

SYSTEM 5: SALES

fit. Failure to find out all the right information upfront can have tragic results that wind up with an angry, frustrated client, tons of wasted time, and lost profit for the agency.

This four-point process is used for streamlining your agency's prospect qualification more efficiently and effectively. By implementing N.B.A.T. you will stop wasting time on tire kickers or clients that aren't in your sweet spot. When you work only with those clients who are the right fit for your agency you'll be able to stop wasting time on those who are not.

N – Need:

Pay close attention to this because it is key in making a good match from the beginning. You need to know what your prospect's needs are and whether your agency's core services will meet those needs. Be direct when you're speaking with a new prospect and ask specific questions to fully understand their needs. What end results are they hoping for or expecting? Find out what success looks like and how it's measured. Ask how the project fits within the overall company vision. Don't try to sell what you want them to want, and conversely don't agree to doing something that isn't part of your agency's core service. It's OK to turn down work if you aren't confident in its potential for success.

Along these same lines, you want to learn the 3 I's from your prospect. The 3 I's dig a little deeper into understanding the Issue, Impact, and Importance of the client's problem. Fully understanding the 3 I's will give you ammunition as you qualify your prospect and again in the future as your measure its success. The 3 I's can also be used as a follow-up tool.

- Identify what **ISSUE** the client believes created the need for your service. Sometimes the "issue" and "need" don't align. As the trusted advisor, you have a specialization and unique perspective to make a recommendation that solves their issue.

- Get a full understanding of the **IMPACT** the issue makes on the client's business. What is the issue costing the client in terms of revenue or new customers? What is a lead worth to them? What is the lifetime value of their customers?
- Learn the level of **IMPORTANCE** this issue has in the big scheme of things. Are there issues that have greater significance? Determine the consequences if the issue is not resolved. Are they losing customers, opportunities, or profit by not working working toward a solution?

Asking the right questions and gaining a comprehensive understanding of the prospect's need will help you both qualify them, as well as nail down the right solution.

B – Budget:

Ask for the the budget straight out. More often than not, you won't get an actual number. At some point in the history of sales, asking for the budget became a game. Most prospects think when you know the budget amount you're going to screw them on pricing. In reality, you need to know their budget so you can determine if you're able to help achieve the desired results while being mindful of their financial constraints. It's like when a real estate agent takes you to look at homes. They've got to know your budget so they don't show you a $1 million dollar house when your budget is $250,000.

I've found two successful approaches to the budget conversation. In the past, I've had countless prospects reluctant to share their budget for whatever reason, but when I started handling it in one of these ways, it became a lot less awkward. You can pick one and tweak it to fit your own personality.

1. **Be the reverse auctioneer.** This can be a great tension breaker because you can insert a little humor if it's appropriate. What I would do is start with an astronomical number and work my way down to something the client can agree to. For example, if you

know you're quoting a $20,000 website project, say something like "Oh, you don't have a budget? I'm sure you do! What is it, like $100,000?.... $75,000?... $50,000?.... $40,000?..." Just slightly pause in between each number and keep working backwards until you reach something they can agree to. They might even chuckle a little at the obscenely high starting figure.

2. **Turn on the sarcasm.** When you're talking to a prospect who is coy about answering the budget question, say something like: "What? No budget? That's awesome! I LOVE working with people that don't have a budget. That means we can spend some time and money testing several ideas before we commit to fully developing just one." Sensing your sarcasm (or possibly missing it entirely) they'll squirm a little and give you at least a ballpark or range you can work with.

Before quoting a project, you must have a budget in mind. If they can't afford your services, don't negotiate down to a lesser level of service or drop your rates in the hopes of making up the loss on a future project. Instead, refer them to another shop that can serve them within their budget. Be helpful. It will earn their appreciation and respect. It might even earn you some future business from them down the road. If the person you're working with honestly doesn't know the budget, that means you aren't talking to the right person. Next step - get the right person in the room.

A – Authority:

Can the client clearly articulate the objective of the project? If the person you're talking to has no idea what the goal and benefit of the project is, you're talking to the wrong person. Were they able to answer the questions about Need and Budget? If not, and they gave you a name or two of other people within the organization, then you know who you really need to be talking to.

Don't spin your wheels working with someone who doesn't have the authority to give you direction or approval. Do what you can to get the rest of the decision-makers involved in the conversation. And don't be deceived by job titles - even the CMO has a boss.

T – Timing:

Can you complete the project within their timeline? Not having the time or resources to complete a project within the client's timeframe means you shouldn't take the project. Only you know what you can do and how long it takes. You might really want or even need this project but if the timing has unrealistic parameters you are setting yourself up for failure. If you knowingly take on a project that you can't complete on time, you'll be mad, your team will be frustrated, and the client will be pissed. A happy client might tell someone how great you are, but a pissed-off client will tell *everybody* how terrible you are.

Lesson 5.2: Managing Sales Stages

Some people will tell you there are anywhere from five to seven stages in the sales process. However, I argue there are only three relevant to the agency industry. In this lesson, you'll learn why I teach three sales stages:

But, first things first. Do you use CRM (Customer Relationship Management) software? If not, you should be. It is the absolute best way to manage… well… customer relationships, obviously. :) If implemented properly, it can be one of your most valuable assets.

CRM applications are popular small business tools because they conveniently and instantly organize customer data from various channels. You can track all your customer interaction from account history, client communications, internal communications, and data on key contacts all in one place. Plus, marrying your accounting software with your CRM can further maximize its efficiency.

Recent studies suggest agencies using a CRM to its fullest potential can increase business up to 29%. The key is using it to help you work smarter and not harder. Some tips for successful CRM implementation:

1. **Keep it simple.** Software that is too complex will make things harder on your team. Likewise, don't try to track too much information. When things are hard people don't do them. If your team isn't using the CRM it's pointless to have one.
2. **Make sure it integrates.** You don't want your CRM to be an island of it's own. Make sure it integrates with the rest of your systems so you can import and export data easily.
3. **Train people on it.** And keep training them as updates are made. Make sure your CRM system makes it easier for your team to get their jobs done, not harder. See #1 about how people do when something is hard :) It's OK to identify proficient users but the entire team needs to use the CRM, from top to bottom.

By implementing an effective CRM system, you can get a clear look at your pipeline and begin to discover patterns in your sales stages. Consider tracking these three phases of sales in your CRM:

<u>Stage 1</u> - When you or your sales team has converted a lead into an opportunity. The lead is already educated on who you are and what you do. There is mutual interest in working together and the benefits of your agency's skill is evident. You are aware of the **N.B.T.** (Need, Budget and Timing) but you have not necessarily met with the **A.** (Authority). **Goal: 25% close rate.**

<u>Stage 2</u> - You/your salesperson has had physical conversations and covered all the bases of N.B.A.T. Your agency fully understands the prospect's 3 I's (Issue, Impact, and Importance) and has gotten the green light to create a proposal. (I caution you not to waste time on a proposal any earlier.) **Goal: 50% close rate.**

<u>Stage 3</u> - Proposal time. First create and then present to the client directly. I repeat, Present. The. Proposal. In. Person. Don't email it off

and hope for the best. More on this later but never, never, never send a proposal without walking your prospect through it in person or over Skype or Facetime, or over the phone - whatever it takes. **Goal: 75% close rate.**

What's really great about tracking your sales progress this way is that you can start planning workload and cash projections 30, 60, and 90 days out. You can use this information when determining your 90-day Financial Goal. You can drive your sales meetings with this data and use the close rates to incentive your sales team. Most importantly, you can use your CRM software to tag prospects stuck in Stage 1 and consider them low-hanging fruit in your outbound efforts. As they say, "the fortune is in the follow-up."

Lesson 5.3: Creating Proposals that Win

Winning more business isn't just about the right pricing. It's about getting your prospect to *want* to work with you. It's about making them realize that with your agency as Alfred, they get to be Batman. In order to get them to believe that, you need a proposal that knocks it out of the park.

I like to think of an agency new business proposal like a phone number. You have to have all the digits in the right order to get the desired result. Below you'll find the sequence of my agency's proposals that converted 80%+.

Creating a template with all parts of my proposal will save you time in the long run. When you get really efficient at creating proposals you will save time for what's really important - growing your business. I recommended creating a master template with everything you see below, as detailed as possible. Each time you create a new proposal, you can eliminate the pieces that are irrelevant and do a find/replace for things that are customizable. You'll get into your own groove and eventually you'll spend no more than 15 minutes per proposal.

As you grow, you will want to look into proposal software. Using technology to create and present your proposals allows your prospects to engage and interact with it. You can use software that tracks open-rate, click-throughs, and even tie automated marketing to it. Of course, old school proposals are still pretty awesome too.

The real key is presenting it in person so you can spell out the finer details and handle objections as they arise. **Proposals have to be presented in person.** This is non-negotiable. If you are at the proposal stage with a prospect, you must make them aware upfront that your policy is to present the proposal in person, via phone, or video conference. Handling the proposal this way will allow you to demonstrate your full knowledge of project scope as well as your strategy for helping the client overcome their problems, issues, and challenges. It also provides you with the opportunity to overcome any objections that may arise along the way. You must be willing to walk away from anyone who won't agree to this term because chances are, if they won't make time to meet with you they're not serious about working with you anyway. You'll see a dramatic increase in your conversion rate when you walk away from price-shopping tire kickers and only spend time on serious, motivated prospects.

Repeat after me: "I will never, ever email my proposals."

The other major key in winning more proposals is having them arranged in a specific order. Most agency proposals start with accolades and bragging points. It's tempting but don't do it. Remember it's not about you and you're not the hero in this story. So just bury that stuff later in the proposal. When you are walking a prospect through a proposal all they care about is themselves, their problem and how it's going to be solved.

The proposal outlined below is presumably presented in person. All the accompanying advice assumes you're meeting face-to-face, by phone, or video conference.

Without further ado, here's how it's done:

SECTION 1: COVER LETTER

Often overlooked but imperative to your success, the cover letter is the like the homepage of your proposal. The cover letter acts as a point of reference when your prospect is re-reviewing the information. In general the cover letter summarizes the engagement and gives a brief overview of what *advisory roles* your agency will play.

SECTION 2: EXECUTIVE SUMMARY

A lot of people treat the Executive Summary as if it is a summary of the proposal itself. However this section explains why the client should select your agency. The rest of the proposal substantiates the Executive Summary with details and evidence to support its claims. Although it's presented as a piece of the proposal, a well-written Executive Summary is able to stand on its own. It sells your agency to the client without them having to read the rest of the proposal.

You'll spend the most time preparing the Executive Summary. Despite the fact that you might have a master proposal template, this is the one document that you should be very careful to customize to the exact project/client you're pitching.

Begin your Executive Summary with a little bit of "neurolinguistic programming." In other words, use psychology to help them buy into your plan and steer the decision-making process. You'll need to use two obvious truths to draw an undeniable conclusion. Start by saying something like:

Obvious truth #1:	Drawing more visitors to the website,
Obvious truth #2:	Increasing sales conversions,
Undeniable conclusion:	Will bring in more revenue.

Example: *"If we can draw more visitors to your website and increase your conversions, we can bring in more revenue for your business."*

There are **4 key elements** to an effective Executive Summary. And you've already done a bunch of the leg work… look back at your Positioning Script exercise when crafting this area.

1. **Empathy** - Identify with your customer by showing empathy for their issue, problem, or challenge. Show them you can relate to their situation.

   Example: *"We know how frustrating it can be when your website is not communicating the right message. Most likely, you are losing a lot of sleep deciding how to fix the problem or whether you should keep status quo."*

2. **Alternative** - Talk about how others have tried to solve their problem and then transition to how you are different than others.

   Example: *"You might have tried to write more content with the hopes your site will rank higher on Google. Most of the time this doesn't work. And when it doesn't it ends up costing you a lot of time and money. But don't worry! We've got a framework and a plan that will help you tell the right story. It will drive site traffic and result in increased revenue."*

3. **Objections** - Raise one or two obvious objections and answer the unasked questions. Bring possible concerns to light and help overcome immediate opposition or resistance.

   Example: *"We know you don't want to waste a lot of time, money, and resources on strategies that aren't going to result in increased business. Even if we are not your first choice, you will find that we are the right choice. Unlike bigger agencies who just want to sell you what they want you to buy, we are smaller, more adaptive and understand your goals. We want to help you find the right solution for your business to thrive."*

4. **Call to Action** - Clearly define the next step and ask them to take action. Don't complicate the call to action; keep it simple. Tell them precisely what they need to do next.

   Example: *"The solution to having new customers banging down your door is right around the corner. Make sure you review the detailed plan outlined in this proposal and let's start a fruitful relationship to grow your business."*

SECTION 3: SERVICES & DELIVERABLES

This section of the proposal outlines the categories of your agency's services. The goal is to get them to buy into your process and your solution for helping them achieve their desired results. This is, by far, the most detailed portion of the proposal.

Leave nothing to the imagination in terms of what your agency does and how you do it. This part of the document must encompass all aspects of the project or engagement and also look ahead to issues that may arise along the way. Don't be vague in the hopes that they gloss over your elusiveness. Anticipate questions that may arise when you're not there and leave nothing to interpretation. Done right, the Services & Deliverables portion of your proposal can also serve to upsell or cross sell for you.

A word of caution. While you're being careful to describe exactly what is included in your agency services, be just a careful to describe what is not included. If you're creating a website, spell out the number of pages, the number of languages, the number of revisions, etc. Taking this approach not only keeps everyone's expectations in check, but it also manages the potential for scope creep before it even begins.

Design Process

Our #1 goal for your website is to develop a graphical representation that uniquely defines your business and separates you from the competition. As a result, we can develop memorable user experiences that drive user behavior.

Our design process is uniquely different from other design agencies. [YOURCOMPANY] designers will start with one design concept at a time. This enables us to fully invest our creative efforts on one specific design concept rather than spending wasted time on multiple creative compositions that will not be used. We have found this process brings better value to the client through saving time, resources, and dollars.

Once we have designed a homepage concept, [YOURCOMPANY] will review it with [CLIENT] to gain a better understanding as to which elements of the design you are most favorable and which ones you would like to see revised. It is very important that [CLIENT] be descriptive in this process to ensure the creative team can deliver a design that captures the uniqueness of your brand. If it is determined that no elements on the initial design are perceived well, [YOURCOMPANY] will create another design based on the new direction from [CLIENT]. Once a home page design is approved, [YOURCOMPANY] will design a sub-page.

Deliverables

* Mobile & desktop layout designs of the home page
* Mobile & desktop layout designs of all remaining pages as per the scope requirements

SECTION 4: PROJECT SUMMARY

The Project Summary is precisely what you'd think - a simple summary of your engagement. No frills, no fluff, no details. However, this is the prospect's first glimpse at pricing. I've found it best not to insert pricing any sooner than this section of the proposal. The first three sections are making claims and getting your prospect's "buy in." Once they believe your agency is the obvious choice, pricing won't matter as much. (Pretty much because you already know N.B.A.T. and all that's baked into the proposal, right?) Putting the pricing any earlier in the proposal is a distraction and will kill your conversion rate.

If your proposal includes one time fees and ongoing fees, be certain to separate those out for ease in interpretation. Don't make your pricing structure difficult to understand. Be crystal clear on what you're charging and how. *If you confuse, you lose.* So, for example:

Initial Setup	
Description	Cost
Web design	$75,000
Mobile responsive	$15,000
Content management	$7,500
Search marketing	$6,750
Application scope	$3,750
Setup Total	**$108,000**

Monthly Fees	
Description	Cost
Search marketing	$7,000
Social marketing	$3,000
Web hosting	$100
Continuous improvement	$4,000
Monthly Total	**$14,100**

In your proposal presentation, explain the pricing and then **STOP TALKING**. A lot of agencies think they have to justify their pricing after presenting it. If you did a good job in the Executive Summary and Services & Deliverables sections, it's not necessary. You already sold them on the why and the how; the cost is just a number. If you feel the need to justify the prices, it shows your prospect you don't believe your agency is worth what you're charging. So - explain the prices and then shut up.

Salespeople who talk too much usually suffer from one major problem. They don't fully understand their agency's expertise and therefore undervalue their services. This causes two major issues which can be revenue killers:

1. **Discounting prices** – When salespeople undervalue the services they represent they are willing to discount or negotiate prices.

Doing this undercuts the agency's level of authority, which also deteriorates the client's confidence. Discounting also creates a bargain mentality and sets precedent for the prospects to expect lower than list pricing if the relationship continues.

2. **Talking too much** – Similarly, salespeople who undervalue their agency also end up overcompensating by talking too much instead of listening. They might be busy rationalizing prices or just talking about the agency's qualifications rather than really listening to the prospect. The salesperson who's busy doing all the talking isn't hearing their prospect's needs. This creates a breakdown in communication which results in the client feeling insignificant or misunderstood.

SECTION 5: ABOUT US

This is another classic mistake a lot of agencies make with their new business proposals. We are programmed to think people wants to know all about us before they'll work with us. Not true! First, people want to know what's in it for them. How is working with you going to make their life better? Think of it like being at a cocktail party. If someone came up to you and starting talking about him/herself and the amazing things he/she has done it would be a major turn off (followed by an eye roll). However, if someone starts a conversation by asking you about you there's a more natural flow and eventually you want to know more about that person. That's why the About Us section of a proposal comes after all the other good stuff about the client.

Often in agency sales we feel the need to spout off our credentials and qualifications to convince someone we're worth their time. We want to impress and end up overloading them with information about our agency, our client roster, our creative, our awards, etc. So that stuff goes in the upfront portion of a the proposal. But, nope - **it's not about us!** It's all about them -- until this point. This is where you're allowed to sprinkle in a little background information and educate the prospect on your business and your team.

First, you want your prospects to believe you can support them and guide them on being the superhero in their own story. Then (and *only* then) they're ready to hear your story and what super things you've done. Don't overdo it here. Be genuine and tell the relevant parts of your story. Think about it like a highlight reel. Include your company vision and a little about the founder or CEO. Talk about the team who will work on this particular project and how they are uniquely qualified. Add in any specific, related experiences and/or case study results that are relevant to this project. That's it. Just a highlight reel on your agency - not a feature film.

SECTION 6: CONTRACT/AGREEMENT

It's a really good idea to have your agency contract included with your proposal. As with all other aspects of the proposal, you'll customize it for this client's project or piece of business. It's important to have the contract in the proposal because you are (or should be) meeting with none other than the person/people with authority to make decisions, it should be fairly easy to commit to a contract quickly. If it's not signed on the spot, at the very least the contract will be in the right person's hands. Besides, wouldn't it suck if the client was prepared to sign a contract and you weren't? Having the contract with the proposal displays confidence and asserts initiative.

Of course, if you're pitching a larger client you may be required to work with their Master Service Agreement (MSA) and you'll want to look it over very closely prior to signing. Although I'm no attorney, here's are some things to consider before signing a client-generated contract:

- Payment terms should be in line with your policy.
- Asset ownership should transfer upon payment, not upon idea creation.
- Keep the client liable for costs associated with missed deadlines.

SYSTEM 5: SALES

Whether it gets signed on the spot or not, set your next meeting in the meeting. That's Sales 101 right there. Don't walk out of that meeting without very clear next steps and a date/time to talk again. *Un*acceptable phrases include, but are not limited to:

- "I'll check in with you next week."
- "When can we expect to hear back from you?"
- "Thanks for your time. Let me know if you have any questions."

In my experience, the only acceptable way to wrap up a sales meeting is saying something along the lines of: "Let's setup our next meeting for a week from today. How's 10AM?"

Lesson 5.4: Increasing Your Chances for Yes

GET INSIDE THE PROSPECT'S HEAD

The starting point of most proposals focuses on an agency's service offering. Unfortunately, providing a full list of offerings can be overwhelming and confusing to potential clients. It doesn't help them decide whether or not to work with an agency. Instead, the focus needs to be placed on the client's existing knowledge base. In order to provide that, you need an in-depth understanding of what's going on inside their head - business environment, objectives, relevant status quo, issues, challenges and more. Today, prospects are frazzled and pulled in many directions, so you won't get a second chance to present the proposal in a format that's easily digestible.

Buyers Matrix Worksheet

If you can dig deep to sleuth-out additional information it will benefit your potential in winning more sales pitches. In order for you to be successful in attacking your sales you have to understand the full scope of the variable that will go into a client's decision making process. After you identify the primary people involved (these are the "Authorities" from N.B.A.T.) the next step is to complete a Buyer's Matrix for each one. The word matrix means "the point from which something takes form or develops"—which is exactly why it's necessary to do this exercise before you get too deep into the quoting/proposing a project. The Buyer's Matrix provides the foundation for an agency's sales attack strategies. Plus, it enables you to get inside your clients' heads so you can better serve their needs.

Begin by answering these questions in as much detail as possible.

1. Roles & Responsibilities:
   - What is he/she in charge of for their business?
   - What area of business is he/she expected to manage?

2. Business Objectives & Metrics:
   - What does he/she want to achieve?
   - How is success measured?
   - How is she/he evaluated?

3. External Challenges:
   - What external factors might make it more difficult to reach his/her objectives?
   - Are they any industry trends that create an obstacle for him/her?

4. Strategies and Initiatives:
   - What likely strategies and initiatives are in place to help achieve his/her objectives?

5. Internal Issues:
   - What probable issues does the organization face that could prevent or hinder goal achievement?
   - What weaknesses in their own processes or systems create a challenge for him/her?

6. Primary Interfaces:
   - With whom does this person frequently interact?
   - Who are their peers, subordinates, superiors, and outsiders with whom he/she frequently interacts?

7. Status Quo:
   - What's his/her "status quo" relevant to your product, service, or solution?

8. Change Drivers:
    - What would cause him/her to change from the status quo?
    - Are there any incentives that would motivate a change?
9. Change Inhibitors:
    - What would cause him/her to stay with the status quo, even if he/she is not happy with it?
    - What obstacles (circumstances, situations, or people) stand in the way of moving away from status quo?

Investing time to create a buyer matrix on each prospect, prior to your meeting, will help you wrap your head around what's going on in their head. Then you can tailor your proposal or presentation by addressing the underlying psychological factors which play an important role in your prospect's buying decision.

OBJECTION HANDLING

A really knock-it-out-of-the-park agency proposal answers questions before they're asked. Be transparent in sharing your exact process to build more trust. Of course, questions will still be asked and objections will still be raised. That's when a salesperson needs to turn into a mind reader and determine if this prospect has genuine concerns or is just putting you off. If there are real concerns he/she needs to do a better job of addressing them upfront. If they're putting him/her off, then the qualification process has failed. (Always remember, there are no bad clients ~ only bad a prospect or a bad process.)

I've found there are several reasons serious prospects object to great proposals:

1. **They remain skeptical.** There is a lack of faith that you (or your business) understands or appreciates the challenges this prospect (or their business) faces. They either don't trust you or they don't trust your plan/process. Be very clear on why you are uniquely qualified to guide them toward a solution or ease their pain points.

2. **There is no trust.** There's a lack of trust either in themselves or in you. They don't believe they can achieve their desired outcome utilizing your products or services. You need to demonstrate otherwise by sharing real stories. But don't limit it to just testimonials from past clients; share stories of how their competition is achieving results, or how they made mistakes by not taking action.
3. **Information is missing.** If they don't have enough information, or the right information they can't make an educated decision. You need to spell out your unique selling proposition. Clearly state: 1. the one biggest benefit of the purchase, 2. what separates you from the competition, and 3. evidence to support your claims. Full disclosure is key.
4. **Pricing is a problem.** If you've followed N.B.A.T. and you understand their 3 I's then pricing should not be a problem, but it happens. Address what it may be costing them not to fix the problem that your business can solve. Demonstrate why this challenge or issue should be a priority for them now and help them see that they have the money, they are just choosing to spend it differently. Determine how to move this up on their list of priorities.
5. **Bad timing** - Maybe they've thought about your product or service but don't think this is the right time to pull the trigger. But, success is never convenient. They need you to explain the possible consequences if they don't take action - what will it cost, what won't they achieve, or what can't they do without you?

Now that you understand some of the reasons prospects object to proposals, think about your experiences in past pitch meetings. Write down all the common objections, criticisms, doubts, and reluctances you have come across. Next, script out your response in a way that both addresses and eliminates them. Consider how you can build some of these in the body of your proposal or presentation thereby answering questions or handling objections before they're raised.

SYSTEM 5: SALES

Despite your best attempts, objections are an inevitable part of the sales process. And, on the bright side an objection isn't a "no". So treat objections as a way to continue the conversation. Try these techniques in order to turn objections and hesitations into a "yes".

- Always, **thank them for raising a concern.** Phrases like "great question" or "I'm glad you brought that up" validates the person and helps keep the conversation alive.

- Next, **use empathy to identify with your prospect.** When you address their concerns with acknowledgement and understanding your prospect is more likely to open up and share additional information.

- Ask some open ended questions surrounding their hesitation or objection. Do more listening than talking at this point. **Gather a deeper understanding** - maybe there's more to it than you were able to identify in your buyer's matrix.

- Do more customer education and a **better job of demonstrating the value** your services will provide. Back up your claims with proof such as past client testimonials, case studies with data/results, or proof of success.

Overcoming objections and hesitation isn't easy. It takes patience and practice. But when you apply these tactics you'll improve the odds. Remember, an objection is not a rejection - it's simply an invitation to try harder.

On the other hand, apart from legit objections, there are some pretty typical stand-offish responses you might receive. Here's a list of of them and how I recommend responding. (Naturally, you'll craft your response in a way that matches your style, personality, and character.)

If you hear: "Let me check with my partner."

It should be your process that this person is already in the room. Remember, this is the "Authority" in N.B.A.T., however if they're not in the room try responses such as:

- "Would it be helpful to meet with us together?"
- "What are you going to tell your partner is the most valuable part of the experience?"
- "What is your process for checking with him/her?"
- "How do you normally make decisions for your business?"
- "OK. When can I follow up with both of you, then?"

If you hear: "I'm not sure about a one year commitment."

When relevant, the body of your proposal should include a timeline. Try adding verbiage about the importance of the timeline, how you came up with the timing, and why extending the relationship is important for managing results. You might also say something like:

- "Let me ask you this…. what kind of commitment do you want from your clients?"
- "Don't you want the large predictable income which builds over time?"
- "How can you sell your product if you are not ready to commit to its success yourself?"

If you hear: "Let me think about it."

You can almost always expect this one and it's a pretty broad statement. This is usually someone who has some specific questions they're afraid to ask. Responding appropriately can help you get to the bottom of the real hesitation. Use questions or phrases such as:

- "Exactly what part do you need to think about?"
- "It usually comes back to trust. Either you don't trust us or you don't trust yourself. Tell me which it is so we can work through the trust."
- "Inaction is holding you back. Action leads to transactions. Why are you hesitating to take action?"
- "What if I said success is only dependent on a 1% change? The trick is to discover that 1%."

If you hear: "Let me see if I can afford it."

This is the "Budget" in N.B.A.T. and you should already have a handle on this information. However, if you do find yourself confronted with this type of objection, you can ask your prospect things like:

- "Tell me the financial results you think you would get from this."
- "What do you think it will cost you if you don't make a change?"
- "Let's go back over the past 6 months, what have you been able to do by yourself to address this issue?"
- "How do you think you will get to your goal of X, if you don't invest in it?"

If you hear: "I don't have the money."

Again, this should not be much of an issue when you have a process for qualifying your prospects and resolve to only work with ones who meet your standards. However, you can talk through financial objections by saying something like:

- "So you don't have any money, or you don't have any money for this?"
- "If you want success on this, you may need to sacrifice something."

If you hear: "I'm not sure I have time to dedicate to this right now."

This particular objection drives me nuts! When you have a complete understanding of their 3 I's you can use that to handle objections that relate to time. One of the I's is Importance. So find a way to remind them of the level of importance this project has in the big scheme of things:

- "Success is never convenient. If this is as important as we discussed, I'm sure you can find the time."
- "Tell me the results you think you would get from this and then tell me if you have the time to achieve them."

ACCELERATING YOUR AGENCY

If you hear: "What's your refund policy?"

This is related to trust issues. They either don't trust you or don't trust your process and want reassurance that if it doesn't work they can get their money back. I don't suggest any sort of refund policy, but instead ask them:

- "Is your mind already made up that we won't be successful?"
- "Why do you think you'll need a refund?"

Fact is, fence-sitters and worry warts are going to be on the receiving end of your pitches. But when you employ the techniques and tactics above you can and will move more conversations in the right direction, increasing your chances for a "yes."

Lesson 5.5: Following-Up After a Pitch

It's true that the fortune is in the follow-up. However, what they don't tell you is there's a right way and a wrong way to follow-up. In order to be most effective and have productive follow-up conversations: **Stop "touching base"!**

"Touching base" or "checking in" is the #1 biggest sales mistake you can possibly make. It is seriously the worst thing you can do with a client who you've already successfully qualified and pitched. Honestly, I have always struggled to find a decent alternative for "touching base" because the call is much more than a breezy check in. "Touching base" is what friends and relative do on occasion. You aren't a friend - you are service provider and authority in your field.

When you leave messages like this, your prospect deletes them in a nanosecond. Worse yet, they see you as just another pesky salesperson. Clearly, not the result you're going for! Here's the deal. To keep sales momentum alive, you need to provide value upon every interaction -- even if it's a quick follow-up call. That means you need to rethink your entire callback strategy.

Rather than just touching base, try one of these strategies in order to create an engaging conversation and advance the relationship.

1. **Try to re-emphasize the business value.** Your prospects will only change because of the impact you can have on their organization. Reiterate it and remind them of how you can help. You might say: " John, in our previous conversation you mentioned how important it was to get going on X soon so you could realize the savings you need by year end. Let's set up time to talk so we can get you moving forward."

2. **Share ideas and insights.** Your prospects want to work with someone who's constantly thinking about how they can improve their business. Be that person. You might say: "John, I've been thinking more about how we can help you increase sales (reduce costs, speed up productivity, etc.). I thought you might be interested in what we did with XYZ organization when they were dealing with the same challenge. Do you have a few minutes for a quick conversation?"

3. **Continue to educate** - Sometimes your prospects are still asking themselves, "Does it make sense to move forward with this?" From the outside, you won't know. But you can keep giving them more reasons to want to say yes. You might say: "John, I know it's a big decision to change from the status quo. That's why I thought you might be interested in this __fill in the blank__ (i.e. ROI calculator, case study, webinar, e-book, etc.) on the XYZ (replace with a relevant topic). Let's set up a time to talk through your questions."

See the difference? You're still providing *goodwill* and *value* even though they already said they were interested and are just stringing you along while they work through internal issues. Even though they might've told you to check back next week. Even though they told you it was a "slam dunk" and they just needed to get the paperwork done.

Drop the "touching base" and "checking in" mentality and remove those phrases from your vocabulary entirely. Instead of making follow up sales calls, become a real asset in their decision-making process.

Lesson 5.6: Building a Sales Team

Depending on the size of your agency, you will at some point be faced with building a sales team. In my experience, the Agency Owner is usually the best salesperson for the agency. That doesn't mean he/she should be the one doing all the sales. By this I mean the Agency Owner really gets all facets of the agency, is most passionate about the work, and therefore is in the best position to sell. But to truly grow and scale, sales should not be and cannot be dependent solely upon the owner.

In fact, the Agency CEO has five distinct roles within the agency and sales isn't even one of them! An effective Agency CEO should concentrate their time, energy, and efforts on these key areas:

1. Growing and mentoring the leadership team.
2. Being the face of the company.
3. Setting and communicating the vision and direction.
4. Managing the agency financials.
5. Maintaining key relationships.

(You'll learn more about the difference between being an Agency Owner and an Agency CEO in System 8, so this is just a sneak peek.) As you can see, the Agency CEO supports sales activity but the heavy lifting needs to be done by the agency's sales team.

SALES PERSONALITIES

According to Harvard Business Review, a global study on the productivity of 6,000 B2B Sales Reps across nearly 100 companies. The study identified some interesting characteristics among salespeople. Turns out they all fall into one of five persona profiles:

SYSTEM 5: SALES

1. **Relationship Builder:** focuses on building a strong personal relationship across the customer organization. They are people-pleasers and strive to eliminate any issues, complications, or tension.
2. **Hard Worker:** shows up first and is the last one to leave. They go the extra mile and outwork everyone by making more calls or appointments than anyone else on the team.
3. **Lone Wolves:** overly confident outlaw; it's their way or no way. If they don't like the rules, they just don't follow them. Basically, not a team player.
4. **Reactive Problem Solver:** detail-oriented and great at post-sales follow up. They ensure all questions from the sales meeting are answered as soon as possible and solutions are executed quickly.
5. **Challenger:** keenly aware of the industry and business of their prospect. They use this knowledge to take control of the sales conversation. They are not afraid to share their opinions even if it challenges the customer.

Understanding these five sales personality types, can you take a guess as to which type of salesperson is going to help you grow your agency? Right - it's the Challenger.

- Challengers educate their prospects and lead the conversation. They offer the client value, and they sell solutions, rather than features or benefits.
- Challengers can press the client when needed because they have their finger on the pulse of the client's business and industry.
- Challengers come to the table with new ideas for their customers to either make or save them money.

One common problem in agency sales is that the sales team has too many Relationship Builders. Performance-wise, they came in dead last and accounted for only 7% of the high performers. For sure, relationships are important in the agency business. But you have to put your Relationship Builders in the right seat at the agency. Relationship Builders aren't bad employees, they just don't make the best salespeople. Challengers are rock stars in the sales arena. Relationship Builders keep clients happy after landing the business. Consider them for an Account Manager role, keeping clients happy *after* the business has been won.

- Challengers win by pushing the client to think differently; they use their experience to create tension versus the Relationship Builder who focuses on relieving tension by giving into the client's needs.
- Challengers push the client outside their comfort zone and focuses on delivering value, while the Relationship Builder focuses on being likable and avoiding confrontation or tension.

HIRING FOR SALES

Wes Schaefer ("the Sales Whisperer") has said agency leaders should always be recruiting. Don't just look for great sales people when you have the need, keep your eyes and ears open at all times. Recognize great skill when you see it, and just like college football recruiters, make room for an all-star even if you aren't in need of one at the time.

In my experience, the best salespeople are the ones who already have jobs. There are exceptions to that rule, of course. But generally speaking, successful salespeople aren't job hunting. So to find them, use your personal and professional networks as well as business social media networks, like LinkedIn. Look at similar service based businesses and see who's really crushing it in sales. Then reach out to those people by describing the criteria for the role you're trying to fill. Make sure to communicate the agency's vision, strategy for growth, and how that person might be the missing piece.

Wes also says to consider taking it a step further and write very specific instructions on how to apply for the position. Using this tactic serves a dual purpose as it can also be your screening process to weed out the people who can't follow directions. To further screen people, put them through a really rigorous interview process and see how much they push back. I've literally walked into interviews for a sales position and not said a word; I make the candidate run the meeting. It's a sales position - so why not make them sell themselves? If you test this tactic, here are some simple guidelines to follow:

- Don't be the first one to speak, instead make them ask questions like a good salesperson should.
- Give vague answers to their questions so see how much they'll press you for information.
- When they respond to your questions, say something like, "wow, that was a terrible response" just to see if they'll defend (and sell!) themself.

Adopting little strategies like these can give real insight into their personality type and the type of salesperson they will be.

For those sales candidates that make it through your rigorous interview process, I suggest giving them some homework. Task them with drafting a plan for their first 90-days. Some will do this, some won't - which is another way to screen out lazy people. For those who do the homework and you like their plan, hire them and measure their success against it for their first 90 days.

Meet with new sales team members regularly. Initially, expect to meet with a new person daily for the first two or three months until they gain some traction. After the first 90-days, manage activity but pay results. Meaning, manage sales activity by knowing how many prospects are in each of the sales stages, with concentration on Stage 2 and Stage 3 from Lesson 5.2. However, pay a base plus commission that is based on taking someone from prospect to client.

SALES COMPENSATION

When developing your commission structure you should target about 10% of your revenue on sales (which excludes marketing, which is an additional 5% of revenue). A sample compensation structure is below. Use what works best for your agency structure; this is just a guideline and by no means an industry standard.

    5% commission for < $250k
    7% commission for $250 - $500k
    10% commission for $500k - $1m
    12% commission for $1m +

For example, under this commission structure, a Sales Rep who sold $502k in new business would be paid like this:

(5% of $250k) + (7% of $250k) + (10% of $2k) = $30,200 in commission

Also, a word of caution: **don't compete with your sales team.** It's tempting because you're an entrepreneur and you love the hunt/kill. Resist the urge to compete with your sales team by giving them all the leads. I know what you're thinking and you're right. You *can* do it better. However, that's not the point. Let them work new leads and let them score or fumble. Celebrate their wins for added encouragement and motivation. Use their losses as teaching moments so your team can become better as a result. Be their coach and their biggest cheerleader, not their competitor.

SYSTEM 5: SALES

Recap: System 5 - Sales

Sales isn't just selling. It's about getting in front of the right people, at the right time, with the right mindset. This section explains how to prequalify prospects and determine any underlying considerations prior to presenting the proposal, as well as how to have the right sales team in place.

▶ **Lesson 5.1: Qualifying Prospects**

Finding out the right information upfront is the key to avoid having an angry client, frustrated team, and tons of wasted time and lost profit for the agency. Adopt N.B.A.T. strategy in order to prequalify your prospects.

N = NEED

You must find out your prospects desired outcome is for the project. Accomplish this by learning the 3 I's: Issue, Impact, and Importance.

B = BUDGET

Don't move forward unless there's a clear understanding of the project budget. You don't want to present a $100,000 solution when there's only a $20,000 budget. Two great strategies for starting the budget conversation with a client who claims "there isn't a budget" - Reverse Auctioneer or Sarcasm techniques.

A = AUTHORITY

Always speak with the decision maker. If you are in an initial meeting asking questions and your contact person doesn't have all the answers, they aren't the decision maker. Save time and headaches by working with the person/people who have authority in the organization.

T = TIMING

Work within realistics timelines and don't over promise just to win the job. Under-delivering and disappointment will only result in a negative experience by both parties.

▶ **Lesson 5.2: Managing Sales Stages**

I recommend using a CRM to manage and track the sales pipeline. Categorize your prospects in three stages:

Stage 1 - When you or your sales team has converted a lead into an opportunity. Goal 25% close rate on all prospects in this stage.

Stage 2 - Your sales team has had physical conversations and covered all the bases of N.B.A.T. Goal is to close 50% in this stage.

Stage 3 - The proposal gets developed and then presented in person to go through in detail, answer questions, and handle objections. Goal close rate is 75%.

▶ **Lesson 5.3: Creating Proposals that Win**

Every proposal needs to have these sections, in this order:

- Cover Letter
- Executive Summary
- Services and Deliverables
- Project Summary
- About Us
- Contract/Agreement

▶ **Lesson 5.4: Increasing Your Chances for Yes**

There's a certain level of psychology involved in increasing your chances for converting prospects in clients. Profiling your client using the Buyer's Matrix Worksheet (included in this section) is one way of getting a deeper understanding and enables you to present a proposal that addresses underlying psychological factors that play a role in the decision-making process.

Preparedness for objection handling can also increase your potential for a sale. Be prepared with responses to comments/objections such as: "Let me check with my partner," "Let me see if I can afford it," or "I don't have time for project this right now."

▶ Lesson 5.5: Following-Up After a Pitch

Three words: Stop touching base! Instead of "checking in" after a pitch meeting, call with a purpose. Provide additional value, share new insights or ideas, and continue to educate your prospect.

▶ Lesson 5.6: Building a Sales Team

Takeaways from this section include understanding the 5 types of sales personas: Relationship Builders, Hard Workers, Lone Wolves, Reactive Problem Solvers, and Challengers and learning which type is best for agency sales… which is the Challenger.

Sales compensation can work in a number of ways; however, a tiered structure can be very motivational. A tiered commission example might look like:

> 5% commission for < $250k
> 7% commission for $250 - $500k
> 10% commission for $500k - $1m
> 12% commission for $1m +

Pro tip: don't compete with your sales team. It's tempting but let them do their job, celebrate their wins, and use their mistakes as teaching moments.

Get more tools, instructional videos, and agency document templates at TheAgencyPlaybook.com

SYSTEM 6

Delivery

ACCELERATING YOUR AGENCY

Driving more leads and converting more opportunities means nothing if the delivery process sucks.

If you're reinventing the wheel every time a slightly different project arises, you need to tweak your delivery. Up until this point, we've covered ways to get clear about your agency's focus and drive more business to it. However if your fulfillment process is flawed or delivery is lackluster, your profitability and future growth is bound to suffer. System 6 is all about streamlining your agency processes and doing more with less.

In this chapter, you'll learn:

1. The detailed processes to deliver a seamless client experience.
2. What documents are necessary for running an efficient agency.
3. How to be more efficient and profitable.
4. What you can do to minimize and prevent profit leaks.

Lesson 6.1: Streamlining Delivery

How many times do you think you craft the same email, have the same conversation, or sit in the same meeting? You don't have to reinvent the wheel with every new project or client. Instead, create efficiencies in your process by streamlining delivery. With the right system, processes, documentation, and communication, there's very little room for any inefficiencies that develop into profit leaks.

The best way to keep the entire team (agency and client) on the same page is to literally hand them the pages. My agency created a master document we referred to as the Mission Plan. Just as the name suggests it was the entire scope and plan for everything relating to the project. Everyone touching the project, agency-side and client-side, was given the final Mission Plan as part of the onboarding process. Everyone from Billing to Project Management to Creative and the entire client team benefitted from the workflow, expectations, and timing documented in one place. This document streamlined delivery while saving time and valuable resources.

CREATE A WORKFLOW DIAGRAM

To get started, you need to consider the flow of work as it travels from signed agreement through the layers of your agency's process and lands at asset release and final payment. Sketch it out on paper. Understanding the agency's workflow will guide you as you develop your delivery process and streamline internal processes. Taking the time to map out your entire process can be eye-opening. Look for gaps or flaws in your process and work to improve those. Use this to fix holes and improve your processes.

CREATE A MISSION PLAN DOCUMENT

(My agency, Solar Velocity, had an aerospace theme so we called ours the "Mission Plan." Name yours whatever works for you and compliments your culture and vision.)

When it comes to the guts of the document, beware this is not a regurgitation of the proposal. It covers far broader areas and dives much deeper. Rather than an overview on the timing and deliverables, the Mission Plan encompasses the full scope of the project and timeline. It identifies and assigns responsibilities and is an overall enhancement of the proposal itself.

EXECUTING YOUR MISSION PLAN

When you adopt your own type of Mission Plan you'll want your team to fill it out in as much detail as possible first. When ready, have the account team meet with the client to fill in the rest of the blanks. The Account Manager should run the meeting while the other team members interpret the discussion and take copious notes during the meeting. With more detailed client feedback, finish and finalize the Mission Plan to create a comprehensive, drilled down document packed with expectations and detailed information on getting the job done. Once it's final, get the client to sign-off on the the document.

KEY AGENCY DOCUMENTS

I'm not going to insert any fluff here; I'll tell it to you straight. **You've got to document everything** in order to run an efficient agency. Workflows help you see the big picture so the left hand knows what the right hand is doing. Documents such as a Creative Brief, Change Order Form, Project Approval, etc. are necessary for accountability. Checklists keep everything organized and prevent details from slipping through the cracks.

You can work and manage more efficiently when you have all the right documents in place. Here's a comprehensive list of the documents your agency needs in order to operate smoothly:

Workflow Processes
Creative Process Workflow
Development Process Workflow
New Client Entry Process Workflow
Delivery Workflow Process

Document Templates
Creative Brief Document
Mission Plan Document
Concept Approval Document
Client Edits and Changes Document
Change Order Form
Project Approval & Launch

Checklist Documents
Design Team Checklist
New Project Setup Checklist
File Folder Checklist

AUTOMATE THE ONBOARDING PROCESS

Marketing automation software is an invaluable tool for reaching and educating your prospects. But another way you can use this sophisticated technology is with your new clients. You can use automation in a variety of ways to keep your client and team on track. Automated emails can be used to welcome new clients and set their expectations on the workflow processes. Automated tasks or email reminders can save a Project Manager tons of time spinning his/her wheels on chasing down signoffs. It can trigger your team to invoice the next stage of a project or send the client an email reminder to pay an invoice. Think outside the box when it comes to maximizing your agency's use of automation.

Lesson 6.2: Eliminating Profit Leaks

Profits leaks are a common source of anger and frustration in any service based business. The key is to identify and minimize them, and eventually put processes into place to eliminate profit leaks altogether. When you put every aspect of your business under a microscope it can be shocking to discover all the tiny ways you are losing money. When we investigated all profit leaks at my agency, we discovered an appalling 60% of our engagements lost money due to our over delivering or under billing. Are you inadvertently sabotaging your agency's profitability?

SCOPE CREEP

The best way to eliminate scope creep is to prevent it from happening in the first place. Scope creep is a major profit killer. It eats at your agency's profitability in subtle ways. It's our innate desire to please our clients which results in scope creep and generally means over-delivering or under-billing.

Scope creep usually starts like this… You start working with a new client and the project is going well. Then the client asks for one small change. You think nothing of it. Sure! You can accommodate this one little request. Then the client comes back with another request and then another. You agree to these "small changes" to keep the client happy and avoid confrontation. As the project continues to grow in size, the client is assuming it will still be delivered within the timeline and budget discussed in the proposal stage. But instead all these changes result in a delay and more man hours. Sounds all too familiar, I bet.

Fortunately, there are a number of strategies you can follow to keep scope creep from derailing your agency's growth and profit.

Eliminate surprises upfront.

Asking the right questions beginning on day one can minimize the potential for scope creep and save you huge headaches in the long run. Knowing and fully understanding expectations, measures of success, as well as being honest with yourself about your agency's capabilities, will reduce your susceptibility to profit leaks. Make sure you've asked, answered, and documented all of these:

- What does the client define as success for this project? How will your client measure this project's success?
- How will your agency's success be measured? What are the biggest challenges of making the project successful for you and for the client?
- What are the expected timelines? Are there any crucial things you should be aware of in advance? What outside forces might create delays in the timeline?
- What is the budget? Can you achieve the expected result within this budget?
- Is this a project that can be successful? Does your agency have the skills necessary to make this a success?

Follow your processes and checklists.

Have you ever seen all the buttons and switches an airline pilot has to thoroughly check before he can fly the plane? What is the first

SYSTEM 6: DELIVERY

thing he does before take off? He goes through a series of checklists and processes - flipping switches on and off, checking lights, buttons, sounds, equipment... It doesn't matter if he's a seasoned pilot with thousands of flight hours logged, all pilots go through the same flight check process every single time. This is the same type of routine you should establish in your agency. You can reduce profit leaks by streamlining everything from onboarding new clients to turning over assets and billing. When you streamline, you minimize confusion and close the gaps where profit leaks inevitably occur. Checklists and processes should include:

- Onboarding new clients
- Starting a new project
- Workflow of the creative process
- Workflow of the development process
- Asset delivery
- Project hours tracking and billing

Document everything.

Documentation doesn't just C.Y.A. - it protects the client too. The ultimate goal of documentation and client sign-offs is to keep everyone on the same page. It all starts with having a detailed, signed proposal with all of the deliverables clearly laid out and the timeline for each deliverable. Next, at every major milestone throughout the project, you should require additional signoffs. Some project milestones at which you should consider obtaining client signatures include:

- The proposal
- Project strategy document
- Concept approval
- Final round of edits
- Final project

In my agency ownership experience these five signatures saved us tons in terms of potential lost profit. When we'd have a client ask for something way off grid, I was able to go back to the detailed proposal and show them what was within the scope of the project. Anything outside scope could be done for an additional fee. Once we started doing this, we went from losing money on out-of-control projects to hitting 30% margins on our projects.

Track everyone's hours.

It's a complete pain in the butt, I know. And your team hates it, I know. But if every single employee is not tracking hours, your agency is losing money. You can't afford to make assumptions on how your team is spending their time. Using time tracking software is an absolute must for getting the profit margins you want. As I said, my agency was losing money on a shocking 60% of our projects and didn't realize it until we started analyzing every aspect of the business. We found we were losing money on hours because we didn't track them and compare our estimates. Neglecting to track hours hurts the profitability of the project and cripples your ability to accurately estimate similar projects in the future.

Whether you're already tracking time or not, here's a checklist you for making sure the efforts are as effective and efficient as possible.

1. Use time tracking software. Since software and technology change swiftly, an up-to-date list of my favorite tools, including time tracking can be find at http://jasonswenk.com/tools.

2. Track your team's hours and make sure you debrief with them after projects. Did they go over or under in certain areas? If so, why? How can you prevent overages in the future?

3. You'll be astonished at what you learn when you see where you're losing hours. Apply your learning and knowledge when estimating hours on future projects.

4. When you get really good at scoping, consider ways to incentivize your team based on hours. How can you structure

a bonus program for hours saved? What other ways can you motivate efficiency?

Even though you are tracking hours **never, never charge by the hour.** As you and your team get more efficient, you will LOSE MONEY. Lesson 3.3 is all about pricing models, so if you skipped or just skimmed through it be sure to check that out.

Expect some scope creep.

I would be lying if I said I had completely eliminated scope creep at my agency. If you expect it and you have a solution for it, you can dramatically reduce the effects of scope creep. For example, limit the client's access to your team. Creatives and Product/Development team members can be in on meetings but all communication should be limited to the Project Manager or Account Manager. I've found clients with direct access to others on the account team tend to bypass their PM or AM for small requests, revisions or tweaks. They think they're doing everyone a favor by skipping the middleman. However, giving clients access to a team member whose time is billable means the client is wasting billable time on a non-billable task. Every five minute phone call or ten minute tweak really can add up. Your team members with specific billable skills should only be working on billable tasks leaving Account Management to manage clients. Those lost or inexplicable hours translate into major scope creep. So minimize the occurrences in order to reduce its effects.

Bottomline, you can keep clients happy without over delivering or under billing. It requires discipline, communication, and enforcement of your agency's policies, processes, and procedures.

Recap: System 6 - Delivery

Having the right delivery process in place will result in a seamless transaction with your clients. By streamlining you'll find efficiencies that make you more profitable.

▶ **Lesson 6.1: Streamlining Delivery**

Documentation is the key to success. Start with a workflow diagram to understand all the hands that touch every project: Sales to Finance and Development to Delivery. Here's the list of all processes, documents, and checklists to ensure smooth agency operations:

Workflow Processes
Creative Process Workflow
Development Process Workflow
New Client Entry Process Workflow
Delivery Workflow Process

Document Templates
Creative Brief Document
Mission Plan Document
Concept Approval Document
Client Edits and Changes Document
Change Order Form
Project Approval & Launch

Checklist Documents
Design Team Checklist
New Project Setup Checklist
File Folder Checklist

SYSTEM 6: DELIVERY

▶ Lesson 6.2: Eliminating Profit Leaks

The biggest culprit of profits leaks is scope creep, which is usually due to delivering more than promised and/or undercharging for your services. Prevent scope creep by:

- Eliminating surprises - understand what success looks like for the client and how it will be measured. Manage client expectations by having a handle on the 3 I's and N.B.A.T.

- Following agency processes and checklists - going outside of process always muddies things up. Doing "little favors" outside of the project scope usually leads to more and more favors.

- Documenting everything - all approvals from the proposal to the final delivery and everything in between should be documented.

- Tracking hours - don't charge by the hour but track hours to gain insights on how time is being spent. Benefits include the ability to better estimate on proposals, identify any bottlenecks in the agency, and incentivize employees.

Get more tools, instructional videos, and agency document templates at TheAgencyPlaybook.com

SYSTEM 7

Operations

ACCELERATING YOUR AGENCY

Solid operations is crucial to agency success. Even if you've got everything else totally rock solid this is the area that can make or break an agency. Operations involves your agency's most valuable assets - your team and your cashflow. System 7 encompasses all things necessary for healthy cash flow, as well as knowing how, when, and who to hire.

In this chapter, you'll learn:

1. When it's time to hire and what seats to fill.
2. Proven strategies to increase your cash flow.
3. How to forecast and protect cash flow.

Lesson 7.1: Building a Team

Looking back at my agency, one of the things I wish I did quicker was hire the right people when we needed them. It's just something you're never really prepared for until you're in the thick of it. Owning and eventually growing an agency has a sort of domino effect when it comes to building a team. You start out solo but you get too busy to go at it alone anymore, so you hire a person. You get a new client, you hire another person. Another client, another hire. It's all pretty haphazard. There is a better way!

THE FIRST NEW HIRE

This section is going to be irrelevant to some and hugely relevant to others. In growing a young agency, it seems the million dollar question is always when to hire, and the equally big ticket question is what role to fill first. Obviously hiring is an important and integral part of agency growth. And as an Agency Owner you can learn from others and hear their stories, but it's you that needs to make a decision that is best suited for the growth of your agency. It just takes some careful and honest reflection about the state of the business and the direction in which you would like it to head.

In hindsight, I did it wrong when it came to my first couple hires. So I'll share a story with you as a great example of what *not* to do.

Back when I started my digital agency, the first person I hired was a Designer. I needed help and I wanted the employee's time to be billable, so I could justify the salary expense. I figured they'd do the overflow of work that I couldn't handle while I did design work and sales… (and Project Management, Billing, Operations). It made perfect sense at the time, except it also created a new set of problems.

I am a Designer by trade; I enjoy it and I'm good at it. I am also good at sales. What I dislike and suck at is managing projects and details. Except, since I hired a Designer that's exactly what I was stuck doing. My second hire, a Developer, also couldn't help with managing and juggling. It wasn't until we grew a bit more that I brought on a Project Manager who took an *absolute* ton of responsibility off my plate. This freed me up to develop the pipeline, build relationships, and focus *ON* the business instead of feeling stuck *IN* it. In hindsight, my third hire actually should've been my first hire. Learn from my mistake - here's how:

- Make a list of all the things you're currently doing.

- Take a hard look at the list; determine which things you're best at and enjoy. Whatever those things are - keep doing them.

- The things on the list that you hate and suck at - hire for that. In most cases, it's going to be a Project Manager. Entrepreneurs aren't typically detail-people. We're big picture people and can't be bothered with little things like details. However, for others the best first hire might be a salesperson, which is also a great move for growing the agency.

- Consider outsourcing some of the other things you hate doing but don't fall into the role for which you're hiring.

TEAM STRUCTURE & ORGANIZATION

Individual accountability is key in the structure and organization of an effective team. It seems wrong to put "individual" and "team" in the same sentence (because after all, *"there is no 'I' in 'TEAM'!"* and all that cliché stuff), but it's true. For your business to really grow everyone needs to know his/her position on the team and understand how his/her function affects all the others.

Hiring on an as-needed basis is anything but optimal. But how else can you get ahead in a service-based business? Until you get really skilled at planning and forecasting, you can't possibly know when you'll need to hire more staff. What you can plan is how you'll structure your team, meaning which seats you'll fill and in what order. It might seem a little corny but visualize the agency as big as you eventually want it. You probably have an ultimate revenue goal but what does that look like in terms of employees? Twenty people? Fifty? Whatever it looks like, draw the organizational chart for it.

(Look, I know org charts aren't for everybody. Sometimes, when you're really small, you think organizational charts are "corporate crap" but truly, having a hierarchy or chain of command is another way of streamlining your business and developing efficiencies. In the beginning it makes sense to have everyone report to the Owner/CEO. But that type of structure isn't scalable. As an agency reaches upwards of 10 employees, the Owner/CEO should only have 5 direct reports (or fewer), with those being the department heads or leadership team.

So go ahead and sketch out a hypothetical org chart. If you can visualize the future structure of your agency at its peak, you can use it as your roadmap to fill the seats you need filled. You can also use it to clarify job roles and goals for each position, as well as identify areas where current employees can grow into new roles within the company. Creating an empty org chart will give you a clear look at what the chain of command will look like in the future and can help with your workflow processes as those continue to develop and evolve. So, yeah - dream big and get it all down on paper. If, as you're growing, you discover it's not as practical as it looked on paper, that's alright. It's no easy task to develop the future structure of a business you haven't really grown yet and it's OK to have it evolve as your team and your business changes. The point is to have a rough plan instead of just winging it and hiring haphazardly.

Sample Organizational Chart

There are a variety of schools of thought on how to structure a service-based business. I don't believe there is one perfect cookie cutter model for every agency. There are a number of variables to consider before creating your agency org chart. Things like specialty (do you want to align your people by their specific skill, or by client niche?) and geographic location (do you have multiple offices or a lot of remote team members?) will be a factor in how your agency will run efficiently.

As a point of reference, here's the org chart we used at my agency. As a rule, I tell agency owners not to have any more than five direct reports. I firmly believe in mentoring and feel that no one can fulfill their own job responsibilities and effectively coach/advise more than five others.

ACCELERATING YOUR AGENCY

SYSTEM 7: OPERATIONS

Lesson 7.2: Improving Cash Flow

Let's be honest, growing an agency requires building capital. Every business needs cash reserves to invest back in, or for the unexpected circumstance. There's no one-size-fits-all strategy for building cash but there are several strategies that, when implemented, can improve and increase cash flow. When coupled with the lead generation strategies in System 4, you can build a predictable business.

I know I struggled for awhile with building enough cash to invest back into my agency. It seemed like we were living "paycheck-to-paycheck," so how the hell were we going to get any extra for reinvesting? Operating this way is exhausting and when it comes down to *almost* not being able to pay employees, it's gut-wrenching. This has got to be the absolute worst part of owning a business. The sense of guilt and obligation makes you take on projects or clients that aren't quite the right fit for you. Deep down you know it but you can't ignore your fiscal obligations either. So you suck it up, do the bad project or work with a bad client anyway, and live to regret it.

At my agency, we were guilty of both. We let the wrong clients or wrong projects in the door because we needed the cash. Instead, what we really needed was a better process for forecasting and protecting our cash flow.

PAYMENT TERMS

There's a variety of ways you might currently be billing your clients but for the sake of conversation let's assume you've got typical agency payment terms of 50% upfront and 50% upon completion. Or, 50% upfront, 25% halfway and 25% upon completion. Regardless, it's most likely you require a percentage at certain points during the engagement. But if you aren't assigning hard dates to your payment terms, you're missing a huge opportunity to improve cash flow.

The real problem with these typical payment terms is that delays are often caused by the client – changing direction, stalling on approvals, not providing information, etc. Their delay causes a delay in project completion and you're stuck holding the bag. Or worse, what about projects that fizzle out completely? That's revenue you had planned on but will never receive. However, when you structure your client's payment terms based on hard dates indicated in the project timeline you are within your rights to bill them even though the project isn't advancing. For example, phrasing payment terms in your contract like this will eliminate the ambiguity:

50% upfront, upon proposal approval

25% upon concept approval or "X" date; whichever comes first. (Make sure "X" date is defined in the project timeline and keeps expectations reasonable.)

25% upon project completion or "Y" date; whichever comes first.

Actual contract verbiage (from my agency):

[PRICING & PAYMENT] *The pricing for all Services and Products is listed on the Project Summary. No work will commence until one half of the total for all Services and Products provided under this Agreement is paid and accepted as a deposit. One-fourth of the total amount due under this Agreement is due upon reaching 50% of completion of the project or* **[CERTAIN DATE]**, *whichever comes first. The remaining one-fourth is due upon completion of the project (launch)* **[CERTAIN DATE]**, *whichever comes first. If the total amount due under this Agreement is less than $5000, the total amount due must be paid 100% in advance.*

Collecting funds midway through the project allows you to more accurately predict your cash flow. It also motivates the client to keep the project moving (since they're stuck paying you either way!). When I implemented this strategy at my agency we had some projects 100% paid but only 35% complete. I don't say this to imply that we were screwing our clients out of what was due to them. I say this to explain how it improved our cash flow situation and accurately predict revenue.

Implementing Payment Terms

The key to successful implementation of this payment terms strategy is educating your clients and enforcing it. Be straight with them and explain why your terms are the way they are. Don't skirt around it or gloss over it. Own it. As you're walking through the proposal or contract, point out the project milestones in the timeline and the associated dates. Remember, this policy protects the client, too. It keeps their project on track. (Hint: you can use their 3 I's here, too: Issue, Impact, and Importance. If the project is as important as they say, they'll want to keep it moving.) Transparency on your payment terms with this will not only educate your clients and eliminate surprises on their end, but also build more goodwill and trust in your relationship.

Enforcing Payment Terms

It's a life lesson, really: Keep your word and do what you say you're going to do. If you have payment terms setup as indicated with dates assigned to milestones in the project, then you have to follow-through. Enforcing payment terms is an area in which I see a lot of agencies hurting themselves. There are a couple common reasons, and while they're very noble they don't change the fact that your agency's cash flow should be top priority if you want to grow.

1. **Being too nice.** In an effort to "be nice" agencies don't enforce their payment terms by simply by not sending invoices on the date as spelled out in the contract.

    It goes something like: *"Well, I know things are tight for the client until we get this _____ project up and running."* To that, I would ask- "Is your agency in a financial position to finance your client until they see results?" Listen, business is business and the payment terms are the payments. End of story.

You can always "be nice" and accommodate special circumstances on a case by case basis but let that be the exception, not the rule. If there are special circumstances, let the client come to you and explain their need for special consideration. Then you can decide whether it's worth the potential issues it will cause you with your vendors and employees.

2. **Being too afraid.** When things are already a little tense with a client, agencies hold invoices because they're afraid to send them on time.

"It's just that I'm afraid if I enforce my payment terms the client might get mad and leave." If you're afraid to enforce your payment terms because a client might leave you, then they aren't a good client anyway. Enforce the payment terms and if they want to leave, let them go. You don't need clients who don't stick to their commitments. And you certainly don't need clients who don't want to pay. Besides, why would the client leave unless you weren't the right fit for them either?

Having the backbone to let bad clients walk away is a virtue. (If you're ever in this situation, give it a try. Firing a bad client can feel intoxicating!)

To avoid or eliminate either of the above issues consider automating the process if your agency lends itself to that type of technology. Consider automated invoicing or automatic charges to the client's credit card on the due dates. If not, and you have manually generated invoices, then it's imperative to remove all emotion and follow your process.

If your process is to send a nastygram on the seventh day after a late payment, then send the nastygram. Keep it polite and professional and don't worry about being mean. You're not mean, or unfair, or unreasonable. You're running a business with its own obligations, responsibilities, and liabilities. So follow your processes to a T because at the end of the day, you have good clients who do pay on time and they need your focus to be on building and growing, not on chasing down bad clients for payment.

INVOICE WITH DETAIL

Are your invoices as detailed as they could be or should be? Sure, you deal with this "marketing stuff" everyday. So _you_ know what you're billing for but the same doesn't necessarily hold true for the client. Each client comes with their own unique set of accounts receivable processes and systems. Your direct client contact may not be the only person that must approve your invoice. So, are the services rendered clear to all possible invoice recipients? If the client provided a purchase order number or reference number, is that clearly stated on the invoice?

Every invoice should include a detailed description of what you've done, when, and for whom. Do not send an invoice for "services rendered"; on the flip side, do not send an invoice that is stocked with a bunch of technical jargon. In both cases, the invoice will sit on your client's desk while they figure out what to do with it. This could take days or weeks, maybe longer. Meanwhile as they're figuring it out, your invoice is getting buried beneath other things in the client's "I'll get back to it" pile. At some point, you'll end up making an awkward collections-style follow-up call to inquire on the invoice. You'll verbally go through the invoice in detail and it will get approved. Then, it will get sent to accounts payable who may take 30-60 days to cut checks. This translates into 90-120 days from the time the invoice is drafted until it gets paid, which is not ideal for your agency's cash flow.

Instead, provide a detailed description of the work you've provided and be sure it matches the proposal or estimate. The more detail the better. You'll never hear a client complain that your invoices are _too_ detailed. If there are any overages be sure you call those out on the invoice with the name of the person who approved it. This is another place where transparency is key. This will speed up the invoice approval process and keep it from sitting at the bottom of a stack waiting 30, 60, 90 days for payment. Everyone has an "I'll get back to it pile" and you want to keep your invoice out of the one sitting on your client's desk. If it ends up there, there won't be any action on it until the client is faced with one of those difficult "collections" calls. (Which is one of those tasks that takes you or a team member away from the real agency work.)

INCREASE PRICES

It seems obvious that an increase in pricing will have impact on your cash flow. However, one of the huge challenges of owning an agency is knowing how and when to increase pricing. You're afraid of losing business by outpricing yourself but you know your work is worth more. And you're so right. It boils down to understanding the value your agency provides and the market's willingness to pay for it. Anytime your agency is in a place where you're constantly too busy, it's a sign that it's time to re-evaluate your prices.

Work smarter, not harder. You've heard it but are you living it? Wouldn't you love to see an increase in revenue and profits while being less busy? Wouldn't you love to just take on the ideal clients with the budget to spend on projects that are in your sweet spot? So the question remains: How can you assess value and increase your prices accordingly?

Accurately assess the fair market value of your services. When you're increasing prices you must have a keen sense of fair market value and couple it with an understanding of what the market deems appropriate pricing. For starters, consider the results your project is anticipated to achieve for your client, and what opportunities it will create for them. If you are building a website for $10,000 that delivers the client $100,000 in annual revenue that's right where you ought to be. I advise my clients to deliver at least a 10x value.

Position yourself as a confident authority. Actions speak louder than words. If you waver in your certainty on your agency's value or try to overcompensate for high prices by offering a bunch of justifications, your behavior indicates a lack of confidence. If you or your team undervalues your agency's work, clients will undervalue it too. If you doubt your agency's ability to deliver the client's desired results they will doubt it too. Be the authority your client is seeking and command the pricing your agency deserves. Get over the concern that you might not win the client because your pricing is too high. Be confident in your agency's ability to deliver value.

Low-ticket selling creates overwhelm. It is easy and fun for you to provide excellent service to 20 people paying you $50,000 each. But it is neither easy nor fun (and damn near impossible) to to provide that same level of service to 50 people paying you just $5,000.

With 20 higher paying clients you could make $1 million but with 50 clients paying less, you could only make $250,000. You make 75% less and work 2.5x more. Low-end clients are usually super price sensitive. They're the ones who'll beat you down on pricing, kill you with scope creep, and be a general pain in the ass. On the other hand, the high-end clients will do everything they can to achieve successful results for their project. They understand the value of what you do and will respect your process for getting it done.

People don't buy based on price alone. They have a definitive need but make their purchase decisions based emotion. The more desirable clients, the ones who really want results will seek out and buy the best solution. By not charging a premium price, you are creating doubt in your prospects' minds as to whether or not you can deliver the results they're seeking.

VENDOR PAYMENT TERMS

The golden rule of business is to accurately manage your cash flow. To do this, a lot of agency owners want their clients to pay as quickly as possible, while paying their vendors as slowly as possible. Sounds pretty unfair, I know. Unfortunately, you can't control your receivable but you can definitely have some say in your payables. Did you know some vendors will work with you on payment terms if you make it worth their while? Try to do one or all of the following:

- **Do research to negotiate terms.** Know what your vendors' competitors have to offer and use it in negotiating. If you can get it for less somewhere else but you want to work with a specific or preferred vendor then leverage your knowledge to get better payment terms. I'm not suggesting you ask for price-matching but use your loyalty to your advantage.

- **Guarantee a certain amount of business** within a specific time frame. Instead of requesting a volume discount use the promise of high volume to negotiate more lenient payment terms.

- **Setup automatic payment** with a credit card or electronic fund transfer (EFT). When your vendor understands you are "electronically committed" and they can count on your payments on a specific date, you may find some flexibility on their end. They're in the same boat as you wanting to establish predictable cash flow.

As you are going through your cash flow with a fine tooth comb look for areas where you can cut back or tighten your belt. What *don't* you need? Are you spending money in areas that you could automate or eliminate? Are there perks you can cut back without demotivating your team or affecting your company culture? What can you outsource cheaper without affecting the work quality? When you find the right combination of increasing predictable revenue and planning for expenses you'll notice fewer ebbs and flows.

Once you've got a good handle on your cash flow the next goal should be reserving at least six months of expenses in a savings account. It takes time to build up cash reserves but it's a good rule of thumb to have about a half-year's worth socked away.

Recap: System 7 - Operations

Solid operations is crucial to any agency's success. Having the right people in the right seats, plus a good handle on cash flow projections will lead to operational success.

▶ **Lesson 7.1: Building a Team**

No matter your agency's size, create the organization chart for the size you wish it to be. Map out how each role/department works with the others. Then fill those roles in order as the need arises.

▶ **Lesson 7.2: Improving Cash Flow**

Don't let desperation back you up against a wall. Improve agency cash flow with these tactics:

1. Payment terms should be:

50% upfront, upon proposal approval

25% upon concept approval or "X" date; whichever comes first. (Make sure "X" date is defined in the project timeline and keeps expectations reasonable.)

25% upon project completion or "Y" date; whichever comes first.

2. Invoice with great detail. Avoid technical jargon but give specifics in the invoice which correspond directly to the proposal and always include client's P.O. number or reference ID. Don't let your invoice sit in a pile on the client's desk because they have questions about it and don't have time to ask them.

3. Increase your prices. Understand fair market value and charge what you're worth (see System 3: Offering). Position your agency as an authority - the trusted advisor and price your service based on value. Avoid low balling or discounting in order to beat your competitors.

4. Negotiate smarter vendor terms. Find price breaks by guaranteeing a certain volume of business or setting up automatic credit card payment.

Get more tools, instructional videos, and agency document templates at TheAgencyPlaybook.com

SYSTEM 8

Leadership

ACCELERATING YOUR AGENCY

You're not trying to be someone else's best. Trying to be your own best is enough.

Leadership is simply taking a group of people and providing them structure, allowing them to be creative, and giving them enough guidance and responsibility to achieve the common goal. Yes, some people are born leaders; however, that's not the only way to become a great one. For your agency to blossom, your role within it must also grow and evolve. This chapter will focus your role as a leader - everything from your team's perception of you to your perception of yourself.

As you consider your leadership role in the agency think of it as a personal development journey. It's a marathon, not a sprint. Make everyday your best day with 110% effort. Each day try to improve little by little. Learn from your mistakes and grow because of them. Hold yourself accountable, but don't be too hard on yourself. Have reasonable expectations for yourself and allow yourself a learning curve. If you work doubly hard day after day, you won't be able to maintain that same level of effort and will eventually burn out. Everyone is a work in progress.

In this chapter, you'll learn:

1. The importance of transitioning from owner to CEO.
2. How to incentivize your team without giving them part ownership.
3. Why and how you might want to set up an Advisory Board.
4. Ways to prepare your agency to sell, even if you're not selling right now.

Lesson 8.1: Becoming the CEO

The way you perceive your role within your agency has a direct correlation to your behaviors and ultimately affects the potential for growth. If you *perceive* yourself as the Agency Owner and you *behave* like the Agency Owner, you are *just* the Agency Owner. You might think it's semantics but really, the role you play has a huge impact on the growth of your business.

Owners are still very much in the weeds. Owners are still scrappy. Owners think no one can do it quite as well as they can… And if that describes you, that's OK. But if you're tired of status quo and ready to transition to something more, it's time to fire yourself as Agency Owner and step into a CEO's shoes. What's the difference, you ask? Well, CEOs concentrate on the big picture. CEOs work smarter, not harder. CEOs hire people better than they are and try to never be the smartest person in the room.

I alluded to it before, the Agency CEO's responsibilities can be pared down to five major roles. After going through this lesson, take a look at what you're doing in your agency. Are your days filled with tasks in these areas, or are you spending your time IN the business?

5 ROLES OF THE CEO

1. **Grow and mentor the leadership team.**
   Remember, you should have a maximum of five direct reports. This is because it's your job to help them develop professionally. Have faith that you've hired good people and they are in the right roles. Give them authority to do their job and allow them to be successful. Encourage and empower your team by removing obstacles. Or better yet, show them how to remove obstacles themselves, so they can grow. If you are your employees' biggest cheerleader rather than a dictator, they are more likely to go out on a limb for you, even if they know the limb will break, because they know you will be there to catch them.

2. **Be the face of the agency.**
   It can be intimidating and put you in a vulnerable position, particularly if you're on the shy side or don't enjoy the spotlight. However, it's super important for you, the CEO, to build your

personal brand and become the face of the company. That means following the steps of some big guys, like Gary Vaynerchuk or Richard Branson. These guys have established their personal brand and used it as the foundation to grow their multimillion dollar businesses. The best way to accomplish this is to get past your hang ups, get over yourself and get started. Put yourself out there by publishing content as yourself, posting on social media as yourself, use your photo as part of the brand and feature yourself on the agency website. As you practice and become more skilled in being the brand, you'll find the right angle, voice, and style that suits you best.

3. **Set and communicate the vision and direction.**
   Your agency vision is the intersection of your goals and your values. Vision is not just financial in nature (although that can be a piece of it); it's much bigger than numbers and dollar signs. The scope of your vision should include all aspects of your business, from financial goals to market position and external/internal perceptions. As CEO, you're the one navigating the course for the entire agency team. They will follow you wherever you're going, as long as they know where they're headed. Setting and communicating visions and direction is paramount to business growth, which is why it's a key role for the CEO.

4. **Manage company financials.**
   As CEO, you must have your finger on the pulse of agency financials. This doesn't mean you need to be the person who actually computes the figures but you have to have a good handle on what they are, what they mean, and how they impact the business. You should have a CFO or other numbers-person who can communicate key financials and KPI's to you. By having regular updates and an understanding of agency financials, you'll be able to make educated decisions on the direction of the agency.

5. **Be available for key relationships.**
   You don't need to do the hunting, your focus is the kill. Let your sales team do all the heavy lifting but you be there to seal the deal. Let your client services team work on keeping the clients happy, and only bring you in when they're not. When you're trying to leverage relationships with strategic partners, be available but not the front man. As the face of the agency, the CEO's presence is necessary for maintaining key relationships but unnecessary for daily grind.

A true CEO works *on* the business, not *in* it. As you go about your daily tasks be sure what you're doing fits in one of these five roles so you can transition into the CEO. If it's something outside of these categories, then assess whether or not you are the one who should be doing it. It will take time to pull yourself away from being the Agency Owner and fully immerse yourself into the position of Agency CEO. It will take a concentrated effort and self discipline, giving up some things you want to do in favor of doing things you need to do. It means getting out of your team's way and letting them do what they're best at, so you can fill the five roles of a CEO. Your team looks to you for guidance and direction; you set the tone for the entire agency.

SET THE TONE

Employees take cues, both consciously and subconsciously, from their leaders. In terms of work ethics, training, tasks, managing their own team... there's a domino effect starting with the way you choose to lead your team. If you're always staying late, your employees will feel as if they should be too. If you never take a vacation or sick day, your employees will feel obligated to model that same behavior. Be the type of leader you always wanted to have and let your team shine because of it.

TRAITS OF A GREAT LEADER

"Leaders are made, they are not born. They are made by hard effort, which is the price which all of us must pay to achieve any goal that is worthwhile." ~ Vince Lombardi

You can just tell when a great leader walks in a room. They have a certain vibe about them... They're authentic and confident, right? Truly remarkable leaders have several common traits which they use to motivate their team, which culminates in extraordinary work. To accomplish this type of leadership, you'll need to exude these six traits:

- **Be aware.** There's a difference between agency management and agency employees. A great leader is aware of the differences and sets themselves apart from the employees in order to remain objective and gain perspective on what's going on within the walls of the business. You'll be well respected when you assert yourself as the captain of the team rather than a fellow teammate.

- **Be decisive.** All the calls are yours to make - especially the tough ones. It is important to give your team the authority to make decisions on their own. However, your employees do understand some difficult decisions must be made by you. A great leader empowers their team to make some decisions on behalf of the agency and doesn't hesitate to swiftly make the difficult ones.

- **Be understanding.** Give genuine praise when it's due and address problems or issues with empathy. Don't play the blame game. Use mistakes as teaching moments to help your team learn and grow. When you show your team how to solve problems in the best interest of the agency, they're more likely to avoid having the same issue in the future.

- **Be accountable.** A great leader accepts responsibility for their own work, as well as that of their team. Having and demonstrating this characteristic makes your team feel assured that you have their back. As a result, they'll want to have yours too.

- **Be full of integrity.** Your values aren't always going to align with everyone on your team. But, employees will follow your lead if you demonstrate an ethical workstyle. You'll earn respect and trust for it. When agency leaders embody the company's core values, it's a lot easier for employees to adopt and model the same level of integrity. Successful agency leaders communicate vision, establish culture, and set core values by living them.

- **Be motivational.** Leaders who communicate clearly and often motivate their team and inspire great work. They challenge their employees to reach their goals and provide the tools, resources, and support to help them achieve those goals. Your team will thrive in an inspiring environment, often exceeding expectations.

Overwhelmed by all this? Afraid you can't live up to the hype? Don't be! You *CAN* do this and you *WILL*. Being an Agency Owner/CEO can be isolating and lonely. It's hard to know if you're doing the right thing and you're constantly second guessing yourself. I remember thinking, all too many times, that I was was living the motto "fake it until I make it." I didn't have the confidence in myself - I even wondered if I should hire a CEO since I had such a high level of self-doubt. It's completely normal to feel that way.

When you marry the traits of an effective leader with the five roles of a CEO, it's a match made in heaven. The downside is, you might experience a little bit of depression. As you work toward your goal of transition from Agency Owner to Agency CEO you'll notice your team doesn't need you in the same way they once did. It might be a little disappointing and disheartening. Feeling that way is normal but remember that's exactly what you want. Your team needs to be able to function without your input on the daily operations. As CEO, your time must be spent on the big picture decisions and tasks that grow and scale the agency.

Lesson 8.2: Incentivizing Employees

A lot of agency owners think they need to make their key employees a shareholder in the business as a show of gratitude. They realize they have a key player or two on the team that they absolutely must have in order to keep things operating smoothly. I caution you, however, not to offer up a financial stake in your agency. Now, if you already have a partner that's great… I had a partner for a number of years and it was pretty ideal right up until it wasn't.

If you have an awesome partnership congratulations. However, it's been my experience that at some point in every business partnership, you either know the bad partner or you are the bad partner. That's because businesses sometimes outgrow people or people outgrow their interest or passion in a business. While it has its benefits, partnerships can create their own set of issues. For example, defining roles and boundaries can become a problem. An initial shared vision is one thing but as time marches on and the vision evolves, both partners must be in agreement on the direction the business is headed. Another problem arises when one person is ready to exit the business and puts a burden on the other partner to buy him/her out.

That's why, for those who don't already have a business partner, I caution you against it. Instead, there are a variety of alternative tactics to show respect and appreciation to key employees. You can incentivize your right hand man (or lady) and other rockstar employees while avoiding giving them a financial stake in your agency.

IT'S ABOUT MORE THAN MONEY

A truly satisfied employee thinks, acts and behaves as though they have a vested interest in the company even when their compensation isn't tied to profitability. A happy employee will be efficient and effective in their role which is true for everyone from the custodian to a Vice President and everyone in between. And, believe it or not, there are a lot of things your team values more than money.

If you want your team to feel motivated and be super productive, first try giving them some of the things they want which money can't buy:

- **View respect as a two-way street.** Of course employees want your respect, but they also want you to be someone they can respect. Be moral and ethical in your business dealings so they can feel good about the agency's work and be proud of their role in it.

- **Don't play favorites.** Just like siblings, employees want to feel like everyone is loved equally. Showing favoritism or having a select few employees who always get special treatment or new opportunities creates tension and is majorly de-motivational.

- **Allow them a personal life.** Most entrepreneurs eat, sleep and breathe their business. A dutiful employee will model your behavior even if it's not expected or implied. Your team needs to know it's alright to have a life outside of work and understand it won't be held against them.

- **Set things right.** Every workplace has someone that gets away with being the asshole. Most employees want nothing more than to see the jerk get called out on it. When they don't, most jump to the conclusion that you're weak, lazy, or just as much of an asshole yourself.

Think about it this way, most people aren't actually unhappy with their salary per se. No one ever says: "I don't make enough." Instead, we often hear "I don't make enough *to*... _____!" (fill in the blank with something like: "put up with this!" or "get treated this way!" or "be this stressed out!") You don't have to a pay huge salary when you're providing a pleasant work environment full of appreciation and respect.

BONUS PROGRAMS

At my agency, we were probably paying our team about 10% below market but what we lacked in salary, we made up for in culture, perks, and leadership awesomeness. That said, we did create an incentive bonus program. When you think about it, everyone gets a base salary just for showing up. But having a team who just *shows up* isn't going to help grow and scale your agency. You can motivate your team to go *beyond* showing up with a bonus program that is structure to keep them motivated, involved, inspired, engaged, and empowered to be able to affect the size of their own paycheck. And, if someone has a specific personal financial goal he/she can reach it by earning it rather just waiting for a raise or asking for a pay bump.

At my agency, the incentive program was tied to each employee's 90-day goals. Similar to the owner's 90-day goals (Lesson 1.2), the goals set for members of the team must be **concise, actionable,** and **measurable.** If the bonus structure means paying on performance, it's important to be fair and set goals that are attainable. We made sure employee goals somehow contributed directly or indirectly to profitability so we could afford the pay out each quarter. We also stacked bonuses, meaning other agency leaders bonuses were tied to the bonus earning of their direct reports. So, one of leadership's 90-day goals was getting their people to reach their goals.

It will take time and several revisions before you find the right bonus structure for your team. It needs to be something that fits in your culture and paves the path toward your vision. Some key elements to bear in mind as you develop a bonus structure in your agency:

- **Tiered:** Create multiple opportunities for success by having different levels of achievement. The bottom level being easiest to reach, the middle being for good performance, and the top level being for MVPs (yet still attainable).
- **Equitable:** You'll probably need to have different bonus structures for different departments, but be sure they're even

across the board. Everyone is working toward a common goal, so don't allow your bonus structure to pit one department against another.

- **Simple:** Don't overcomplicate the bonus program. No one wants to feel like they need an attorney or translator in order to understand it. A successful bonus program is easy to understand and leaves no margin for misunderstanding.

- **Timely:** Frequency is key. Keep your bonus structure bound by time, such as 90-day quarters. In the agency business it's not realistic to reward employees every week or month. However, you also won't motivate your team by making them wait an entire year for a performance-based bonus.

- **Reinforced:** Give constant feedback. The reason I teach 90-day goals rather than just annual goals is because you can change courses if you're headed in the wrong direction. Likewise with your team's bonuses; communicate when they're not on the right track. Make sure it's easy for your team to monitor their own progress. Performance bonus results should not come as a surprise.

KEEPING EVERYONE ON TRACK

Sure, leadership meets with the Project Managers, Account Managers, and Sales Team regularly. But what about everyone else? Keeping a team of creative or technical people on track can feel a little like herding cats. But it's super important to touch base with everyone to make sure they're putting energy and focus on the right things at the right times. (Especially when their time is billable.)

I know what you're thinking... "who needs more meetings?" (cue the eye roll). It actually doesn't have to be as cumbersome as a meeting. I suggest daily check-ins at the start of each day. There's a ton of different project management software tools you can use to make sure the entire team is looped in with one another.

At my agency, we'd have each work group start their day by answering three questions and sharing it with their department distribution list via email.

1. What did you do yesterday?
2. Did you run into any issues with it?
3. What are you planning to do today?

By starting each work day with the answers to these three short questions, each person sets up his/her own day with purpose. It's a proactive approach to the day versus the alternative reactive approach. Many of us start our day by checking email and reacting to what we read. Our day is usually driven by whatever is waiting in our inbox. However, when you start your day with purpose - stating what you're going to accomplish - you are the boss of your own day.

This approach is a great way of holding oneself accountable as well as opening communication among teammates. It allows leadership to see what direction each team member is headed in and intervene if they identify a potential issue. It also helps keep other department informed which creates efficiencies in processes and workflow.

For example, let's suppose someone in Development has been working on a project, dedicating full time hours for several weeks when suddenly the Finance group realizes the client's midpoint invoice hasn't been paid and work should have halted. Many, many hours are wasted. That sucks, right? But when everyone's in the loop, Finance would know how Development is spending their days, closing that gap. It's a win in terms of preventing a profit leak. Gotta love that!

KEY EMPLOYEE AWARDS

Beyond bonuses, another way to incentivize is with a Key Employee Agreement. This type reward program is something you can put in place in lieu of giving away shares of ownership. This type of arrangement both recognizes key employees' significance in the agency and protects them in the event of financial failure.

With a Key Employee Agreement in place, the owner(s) identify a person or people who are to be rewarded financially in the event the agency changes ownership. In my case, we set aside 10% of our net value in reserve for key employees. There were a handful of people who had these agreements and therefore, when the agency sold they were paid a portion of the agency's value at the time of sale. For example, of the 10% in reserve Key Employee #1 might be entitled to 2%, Key Employee #2 may get 5% and Key Employee #3 gets the remaining 3%. In our case, we allocated 100,000 equal units (Note: these are "units" not "shares").

Here's some of the language from our Key Employee Agreement. (This is just an example for the purposes of demonstration. Consult an attorney when drafting your own document.)

1. Key Employee Reserve and Unit Awards.

(a) If, during the Term (as hereinafter defined), there is a Change in Control of Company, Company shall reserve up to ten percent (10%) of the Net Proceeds from any Value Exchanged for such Change in Control (the "Key Employee Reserve") and such reserve shall be for the benefit of Employee and any other employee subject to a Key Employee Change in Control Agreement (the "Key Employees").

(b) The Company has elected to divide the Key Employee Reserve into 100,000 equal units ("Units"). In its sole discretion, the Company may award any number of Units to one or more Key Employee(s) so long as the total number of Units awarded does not exceed 100,000.

(c) The Company awards _____ (fill in number) Units to Employee.

(d) On the later of two (2) months following the Change in Control or two (2) months following Company's receipt of all Value Exchanged,

ACCELERATING YOUR AGENCY

Company shall distribute the Key Employee Reserve to all Key Employees in proportion to the number of Units awarded to each Key Employee. Any Units not awarded on the date of distribution shall not be allocated among Key Employees. (e.g., if Key Employee A is awarded 60,000 Units and Key Employee B is awarded 10,000 Units, the remaining 30,000 Units not yet awarded shall not be distributed. The Key Employee Reserve distribution shall be treated as compensation for the Employee, and, as such, shall be subject to all applicable federal and state payroll withholdings, including social security.

(e) At any time prior to a Change in Control, Company may, at its election and in its sole discretion, terminate this Agreement and any other Key Employee Change in Control Agreement.

(f) Key Employee agrees to hold in the strictest of confidence the existence of this Agreement and any information about any other Key Employee Change in Control Agreement.

Lesson 8.3: Determining Valuation

Build your business to sell but treat it like you never will.

Everyone, at one point or another, has given thought to his/her end game. Admit it; it's crossed your mind. "Maybe someday I'll get a crazy big offer from a bigger agency" or "Will my partner buy me out when I'm ready?" No matter how or when it happens, next year or in fifty years, there's one thing you can do to control your destiny: **build a business worth buying.**

Most entrepreneurs are finishers. They think they can't step away until they're finished working. This translates into thinking you can't sell your business until you're ready for retirement. However, in my case, I had met my goal of building an agency that exceeded $10+ million in revenue. I knew I didn't have it in me to do what it was going to take to get to the next revenue benchmark so when the right opportunity came along, I sold the agency.

BUILD A BUSINESS WORTH BUYING

Everyone's reasons for selling are different but a buyer's reasons for buying can usually be put into one of three boxes. Understanding those reasons before you're actually even thinking about selling will set you up for a profitable business now and an attractive acquisition for someone else later.

Agency Buyer Reason #1: To grow and scale more rapidly.

Running a well-oiled machine by having buttoned-up processes and rock star talent is what buyers will notice. A prospective buyer will be attracted to your processes and talent, and they will realize that buying your agency will help them scale and grow much quicker than if they develop the systems or acquire the talent organically.

What you can do now:

Since honing processes and building a talented team takes years, focus on it now. Develop processes that everyone's talking about. Maybe it's your delivery system or your scoping process ... Pick one or a few things and do it or them better than anyone else. Partner agencies, competitor agencies, clients, and industry colleagues will talk. Be famous for it.

When it comes to talent, most small agency owners think they can't afford the best. In my experience, it's really the best that want to work for smaller agencies. There's more autonomy at smaller agencies, and it's easier for creativity to flow when it's not being stifled by corporate procedures, a stuffy legal department, and an HR-enforced dress code. Don't think you're too small to attract big talent. You might be the breath of fresh air that big talent wants and needs.

Making sure you have the right people in the right seats can be a lot of work, and it can only be done over time. Good processes and good talent aren't mutually exclusive. With the right team in place, processes won't be an issue which means you, as the Agency

Owner, can work on growing instead of fixing things. You can be proactive instead of reactive. In addition, your agency's reputation for great talent or great processes in the industry can even land you an inbound acquisition offer.

Agency Buyer Reason #2: A presence in your geographic location.

Sometimes a great agency is looking to expand geographically. Rather than starting at square one and opening a satellite office in a new location, a buyer will look to acquire an agency that's already established in their desired location.

What you can do now:

Make your mark. I owned my digital agency for twelve years, and during that time, we found ourselves on a lot of "top" and "best of" lists -- Atlanta's Best Place to Work, Top 25 Small Businesses, Top 10 Most Dependable Web Design Firms in the Southeast, Atlanta's Top Marketing Firm ... you get the picture. I don't tell you this to impress you but to impress upon you that lists mean something to people.

Build an awesome agency and make sure everyone knows about it. Local titles, awards, and honors will put your firm on the map. It's not the ADDYs that get you recognition, though they're nice, too. Getting your name on these lists is like marking your territory. It makes you appealing to clients, talent, and eventual prospective buyers. Why would a buyer move into your location and compete with you when they could just approach you with an offer to buy you?

Agency Buyer Reason 3: Bigger market share.

It's like the old adage: It's not *what* you know but *who* you know. And just as badly as you want to do good work with big clients, so do other agencies. This type of buyer is either motivated by your client list or they're after more of the dollars those clients are spending (such as a traditional agency that is looking to acquire a digital agency). There are two ways you can grow your business while also attracting this type of buyer.

What you can do now:

Define your niche and appeal to those specific clients. Don't be afraid of it, embrace it. As I've said, niching does not mean turning away business. It means focusing your time, your talent, and your resources toward one type of client. When you establish yourself as a marketing authority in a specific industry, you are also establishing yourself in the agency community as an authority in that industry. When a competitor or an agency who offers complimentary services is looking to grow, they'll look to you as a way of doing so.

When I sold my digital agency, it was to a partner agency that we'd worked with on several other projects. The agency was larger and had complimentary services. In the beginning we were looking at ways to bring each other more business. After a closer look at what we were doing -- our processes, our talent, and our clients -- their leadership presented an acquisition offer. We weren't actively seeking to sell but we got noticed. *Build your business to sell but treat it like you never will.*

DETERMINING VALUATION

Even if you're in it for the long haul I know you've wondered about the value of your agency. In short, your agency's worth is the magic number between the amount someone is willing to pay and the amount you're willing to accept. But the lengthier, technical answer is all about profit margin. Your goal is to be at 40%+ in profit.

You can get a baseline by looking at the past 3 years growth. An acquirer isn't going to look at the details, they want to know that you are trending in a positive direction. If not, it will be a fire sale and you will be stuck taking whatever is offered. To have the upper hand, maintain positive, upward growth percentages year over year. A good range of growth would be between 15% and 50% growth in gross revenue. You also need to look at the profit. Revenue means nothing if you're not paying attention to the bottom line. Whether you're a $10 million agency or $1 million agency, you should be making mad bank from a profit standpoint.

INCREASING VALUATION

While significant profit is awesome, it's only a small piece of the bigger picture. Value is really what's going to get your agency noticed and eventually sold. With that said, there are a number of ways to increase your agency's value. The key is not waiting until you're ready to sell. These are things you should be doing to consistently grow your business and its value. And when you do, you will not only benefit in the short run but you'll also attract the right kind of buyers and benefit in the long run too.

- **Valuable Assets** - Your clients are your only real assets. Totally buttoned-up contracts are super important. The more long term, transferable contracts the better. Transferable means that you can hand off the business to your buyer with little more than written notice to the client. Consult with an attorney be make sure your contracts work in your best interest in terms of a future merger or acquisition.

- **Reliable Cash Flow** - Don't let too much of your revenue be tied up in just one client. Diversify your client roster (by size, not by category) so you aren't too reliant on just one big fish to pay all the bills.

- **Solid Profit** – Be sure you've eliminated and prevented scope creep (Lesson 6.2). Are you under charging? Are you over delivering? Make sure your bottom line is solid by having a handle on scope creep. The best way to increase your value is with a healthy profit margin.

- **Strong Pipeline** – Make sure you have a multi-channel business development strategy. A 3 prong approach (inbound, outbound, and strategic partnerships) is the only way to consistently fill your pipeline.

SYSTEM 8: LEADERSHIP

- **Know the Numbers** – Always have a good idea of your KPIs. You should be measuring and tracking your KPIs such as: profit margin, lifetime client value, burn rate. Not only do you need to know your numbers but you also need to watch them to identify areas for improvement.

- **Outside Perspective** – It's hard to see the forest for the trees. When you're in the trenches, it's a great idea to bring in an objective third party to help you see areas that need improvement. Consider an advisory group, board of directors, or a business coach.

Lesson 8.4: Being Acquired

Whether you're actively pursuing a buyer or get an offer out of the clear blue, there's a lot to know about acquisition. (Particularly if you're completely green to the process, like I was.) In this section, I'll outline the stages of an acquisition as well as some major pitfalls to avoid. You don't want to shoot yourself in the foot or kill a deal by falling in an avoidable trap.

STAGES OF AN ACQUISITION

It can be pretty exciting when someone reaches out with interest in acquiring your agency. But the reality is that it can be a very lengthy process and really difficult if you aren't prepared with realistic expectations. I've broken it down into six basic stages (although there's nothing very basic about it!).

1. **Initial inquiry:** An acquirer reaches out and asks questions about your agency with the intent to make an offer. Your answers determine whether or not they want to go the next step and issue a letter of intent. When the inquirer is asking questions, answer honestly but don't go overboard with it. Don't allow your excitement make you offer up more info than what is requested. It's a very common mistake and never works in the seller's favor. More on that later.

ACCELERATING YOUR AGENCY

2. **Letter of intent:** The letter of intent is an evaluation of what the buyer feels your agency is worth, as well as a high level structure of the proposed deal. Make sure you will be happy with the general terms described in the letter before you move onto the next step. If you're not, this is the time to negotiate some of the major points.

3. **Escrow account:** Requesting a deposit in escrow is a great way to weed out time-wasters. Serious inquirers should be willing to set aside a small portion of the sale amount in escrow. For example, let's say your agency is valued at $5 million and you're taking $1 million cash up from and $4 million in equity over time. You can request the buyer set aside $20K-$50K (so, that's just 2-5% of the upfront cash amount) in escrow now. Then if the sale falls through due to the buyer's negligence, you're entitled to keep the escrow money for your time and trouble. If not, it gets applied to the sale.

4. **Due diligence:** Both parties use this period of time to learn as much as they can about the other. You have just as might right and responsibility to ask the buyer all the same questions they're asking you… from client lists to financials. You'll also want to make sure cultures will mesh, so tour their offices and get a feel for things.

5. **Term sheet:** Following the due diligence phase, the final step is the term sheet. This is the legal document that spells out every detail of the sale. In most cases you'll have a cash amount and an earn out. Enter into the deal with an amount of cash in mind prior to be presenting with a formal offer. Having a number in mind will prevent you from settling for a lesser amount. I also caution people against tying any cash receipts to an earn out. I believe most earn outs are designed to fail. So, expect you won't see a dime of the earn out and be happily surprised if you do.

6. **Final step:** Figuring out what's next. It's totally personal and can

be somewhat scary depending on how long you've been running your own business. This is the part I struggled with for a couple years. Don't stress about it though - the really hard part is behind you. All that's left is to celebrate!

MISTAKES TO AVOID

Was I happy with the sale? Yes. Do I think there were things that could have gone better? Definitely. That's why I like to share some of the common missteps so others can avoid making mistakes in a potential acquisition or merger situation.

1. Helping too much.

If you get an inbound acquisition inquiry it's natural to want to move things along by being super helpful. Helpful is good, but I caution you against being too chatty. You're passionate about your business but don't let yourself gush too much about your clients, successes, strategies, processes, etc. I get it. Your agency is your baby and you're so proud of everything it has become. You want to brag a little (or a lot). Resist the urge!

You definitely need to provide the usual information such as margins, revenue, employees, and a client list. But when it comes to what makes your agency great -- your processes, strategies, and intellectual property -- keep it to yourself. This buyer is probably a competitor in one way or another. Why would you share your differentiating factors with them right off the bat?

Instead of blathering on and on about your awesome sauce, provide only what is asked for and limit it to your core services, full-time employees, financials (such as gross or net revenue, profit margins), and a list of major (not all) clients. *Help without being too helpful.*

Upon the receipt of this information, your potential buyer should draft a formal Letter of Intent. After you accept it, there's a period of due diligence that is meant to protect and benefit both parties.

Use this time to ask questions. Anything they've asked for, you ask for too. Request their financials, employee count, client list, reasons for buying, etc. Take a walk through their office, and get a sense for the culture. Will it mesh with yours? Will it mesh with that of your clients? You can be cooperative, professional, and courteous while still protecting your business, employees, clients, and financial interests.

2. Celebrating too soon.

It's exciting and flattering when there's interest in an acquisition or merger. You'll want to spread the news; however, it's important for you, your team, and your clients to keep it quiet until there is a formal and mutually agreed upon deal. Don't break open the bubbly until all the i's are dotted and t's are crossed. Deals fall through all the time for reasons and circumstances beyond either party's control. Instead, keep the information to a need-to-know basis.

Do you have a partner? He needs to know. Your Accounting Manager or Finance Director? Definitely need to know. A board of directors or advisors? Certainly need to know. Otherwise, stay silent for awhile. Instead of doing a happy dance and daydreaming of ways you'll spend that cash, figure out what the magic number needs to be. Know the cash amount you'd be happy to walk away with and don't let it be tied to an earn-out. Speaking from experience, the seller really has no control over the success of an earn-out, and most earn-outs are structured to be unattainable.

Rather than celebrating too soon or telling too many people, act like it's never going to happen. Imagine the repercussions if the deal falls through and you've let word slip. You'd lose the trust of your employees and the confidence of your clients - major fail and totally avoidable.

3. Checking out too soon.

Keep things business as usual. Don't stop hustling as hard as you always do. Like I said in the earlier section: build your business to sell but treat it like you never will.

SYSTEM 8: LEADERSHIP

If you check out mentally and the deal falls through, you're stuck with a stagnant business, a demotivated and deflated team, and just a general mess. Instead of checking out, be proactive in writing your new role. Are you willing to stay on? If so, for how long? Will you sign a non-compete? If you do, at what length? You'll be needed for a while due to your connections to key client contacts not to mention the overall morale for your team. But you might not want to work for someone else for too long. Trust me, it feels weird!

An acquisition is the goal for many entrepreneurs, but it can also be an overwhelming and stressful time. Then when it's all over, there's a serious adjustment period. What's next is up to you, and that too can be an overwhelming and stressful time. So often we get so focused on making it to the finish line that we lose sight of what's beyond it. When you get to your finish line, don't worry too much about where the next one is. Just enjoy the journey toward it.

Lesson 8.5: Putting it All Together

It's hard to see the forest for the trees. When you're too close to every aspect of your agency it can be helpful to seek an outside perspective. This can done through coaching or mentoring from someone who's been in your shoes, or through an Advisory Board.

Coaches or mentors can be great if you find the right one. You might choose someone with a certain area of expertise - sales or finance. Or, you might choose someone with the industry.

It should be someone who's been where you want to be and whose style and personality align with yours.

If you decide to create an Advisory Board you will want to select people with a variety of areas of expertise. Create a list of the 4-5 areas (sales, finance, marketing, HR, etc.) and then think of candidates who excel in those areas. You might even consider an established or former Agency Owner who can use their experiences to help you grow. Next, think about how the Advisory Board will function. Will you meet quarterly or semi-annually? Where will you meet (weekend retreat, offsite, after hours)? How will you compensate the board (such as pay for the retreat or offer a stipend for their time)? Finally, talk to the candidates and explain what and why you're asking for their help. You might be surprised at how much valuable knowledge you can glean from the experiences of others. And, they'll feel a sense of honor and flattery from being asked to sit on your Advisory Board. It can be a real win-win!

Recap: System 8 - Leadership

Leadership is simply taking a group of people and providing them structure, allowing them to be creative, and giving them enough guidance and responsibility to achieve the common goal. This section is dedicated to advising great leadership.

▶ **Lesson 8.1: Becoming the CEO**

There's difference in being an Agency Owner and being an Agency CEO. A CEO works *on* the business, not *in* it. In order to transition from owner to CEO, leave daily tasks to your team and make these five roles your priorities.

1. Grow and mentor the leadership team. This is just your direct reports which should be no more than 5 people.

2. Be the face of the agency. Your agency is an extension of you so you must become the brand.

3. Set and communicate vision and direction. You're the captain of the ship and as such, you've got to tell the crew where they're headed and then navigate the course.

4. Manage company financials. Have a full understanding of the financial landscape of the agency by knowing your KPIs so you can make educated decisions.

5. Be available for key relationships. Let the sales team do all the selling but be available, if necessary, to seal the deal. Be accessible, but not on the front lines.

▶ **Lesson 8.2: Incentivizing Employees**

Bonus programs are an amazing way to motivate and inspire your team. Successful bonus programs are 90-day goal oriented and their structure is concise, actionable, and measurable. Keep your team on track by making sure each department holds daily meetings or is collaborating daily within project management software.

Don't give away ownership to show appreciation to key employees. Instead, install a Key Employee Agreement. This is documentation that allows key employees a portion of the proceeds upon the sale of the agency.

▶ Lesson 8.3: Determining Valuation

Build your business to sell but treat it like you never will. Even if your end game is in the distant future, you should work to grow your agency's value now. Understanding and catering to a potential buyer's motives will give you an edge:

Reason 1: To grow and scale their existing agency more rapidly.

Action: Hone your processes and build a talented team. Be known for your awesomeness so another agency might adopt the "if you can't beat 'em, join 'em" mentality.

Reason 2: To have a presence in your geographic location.

Action: Be known for being the best in your area. Dominate in your location and make press over it.

Reason 3: To gain market share among your client base.

Action: Identify your niche and establish your agency as the prefered specialist among that audience. That way, when a competitor is looking to grow, they'll look to you as a way of doing so.

Profit is awesome but it's only a small piece of your agency's value. There are several key elements that add up to agency valuation.

- **Valuable Assets** - This means clients with long term, transferable contracts. The more, the better. Consult with your attorney for writing a transferable contract that benefit all parties.

- **Reliable Cash Flow** - Don't let too much of your revenue be tied up in just one client.
- **Solid Profit** – Make sure your bottom line is solid by having a handle on scope creep. The best way to increase your value is with a healthy profit margin.
- **Strong Pipeline** – A multi-channel business development strategy with a 3-prong approach: inbound, outbound, and strategic partnerships.
- **Know the Numbers** – Always have a good idea of your KPIs and are tracking things like profit margin, lifetime client value, burn rate.
- **Outside Perspective** – It's hard to see the forest for the trees. Try getting objective consultation or advice from advisory group, board of directors, or a business coach.

▶ Lesson 8.4: Being Acquired

The merger or acquisition process can be very eye opening. Preparedness can give you an upper hand in fair negotiations and self protection/preservation.

Stages of an acquisition:

1. Initial inquiry - an informal step to garner information.
2. Letter of intent - a formality stating the proposed deal.
3. Escrow account - a portion of the sale price set aside as earnest money.
4. Due diligence phase - time for both parties to do their homework on each other.
5. Term sheet - legal documentation with sale details, including terms and conditions.
6. Final step - deciding what's next for you, the owner.

ACCELERATING YOUR AGENCY

Acquisition mistakes to avoid:

1. Helping too much. Answer questions honestly but don't gush. If the sales doesn't go through you will have given away the secret recipe to your awesome sauce.

2. Celebrating too soon. Keep the sale on a need-to-know basis until you're in the term sheet phase. Sharing with your team or clients can be super demotivating and have serious negative effects should the deal crash.

3. Checking out too soon. Work your business and don't lose your hustle. Avoid spending time daydreaming about how you'll spend your net profit from the sale and keep working the business like you still depend on it.

▶ Lesson 8.5: Putting it All Together

Agency ownership can be lonely. Seek the help of others who've been in your shoes and can advise or mentor but are not emotionally or financially tied to the success of the agency. Options for this role might include Advisory Group or Board of Directors, an outside coach or mentor, or mastermind group.

Get more tools, instructional videos, and agency document templates at TheAgencyPlaybook.com

CONCLUSION

If I could leave you with one final nugget of wisdom it would be to take time to fully understand the landscape of your business and the evolution of your role within it. We often get so caught up in the craziness of the moment we forget to step back and see the bigger picture.

Your actions today will have a lasting effect on your agency for the months and years to come.

When I sold my agency it seemed like the right decision at the time. Looking back, though, the agency might have been worth so much more if I had done things differently and waited a few years before selling.

We were approached by a strategic partner which was another agency with complimentary services. I made the decision to sell because the right offer came my way and I was having partner problems. In hindsight I made the "easy decision" to sell because I thought it was the only way out. I lacked the clarity to see the situation objectively.

If only I'd have faced the problem head on, I could have opted to buy out my partner and reallocate some of the agency's discretionary funds (like the money we were spending to sponsor a race car team!). Those monies should have been used to reinvest back into the business and the employees.

I have no regrets! I love what I do now. But if you can gain anything from this book it should be a level of clarity to see your agency for what it is and what it can be so you can avoid haphazard, knee-jerk decisions, and enjoy growing your agency faster and easier.

DEDICATION

My dad was the biggest inspiration in my life and although he passed away in 2015, I feel he wasn't done helping people, so I wanted to pass this message on to you.

If I could give you just one word to describe my dad it would be FEARLESS. When I think of my dad I think of Superman. I never saw my dad fear anything other than when my parents told me they were getting a divorce. Only then I could sense his fear of how it would affect me - but everything turned out ok.

My dad never told me I could not do something I wanted in life. I think that was his way of helping me be fearless too. I am not talking about saying 'no' to the little parenting things. I am talking about the things I wanted to do and be in my life.

I never saw my dad quit anything. When I was in high school, my dad ran every day in the morning. One time he asked me to run with him. I remember the first time running around Wahoo Road with him. When we started out, he waved to an old man who was walking. When we came back around, my dad was in front a pretty good way and as I passed the old man, he said something to me like, "better luck next time." Even when my dad was not saying something to me, he was helping me. He was always pushing me forward and motivating me to be better.

After my dad beat me that day, I got inspired to get better so I could keep up with him. Over the year, we ran together pretty much every day and chatted about the future. One day I was watching TV and saw a story about a father/son team doing the Ironman together. The son could not walk and was severely handicapped. The father had to tow him in a boat while he swam, bike him on a carriage in front, and then push him in a stroller on the run. It was something so incredible to watch since the father and son were doing this together. When I told my dad I wanted to do the Ironman, he could have said "How can you do an Ironman that's over 160 miles when you couldn't even run 1.5 miles?" Instead he simply said "Do it."

He never said I couldn't do something. He never tried to talk me out of anything other than racing cars. And, I understand now why he wanted me to stop.

My dad was extremely successful in life, from working his ass off for an amazing career to providing an incredible childhood for me. He wasn't just successful, though. He was significant. You see, success just affects you but significance means you positively affected other people's lives. And he did that so many times over.

When I was starting my business, he never offered to give me any money, which I respected. I wanted to start out from nothing like some of the greats we all know. But I realize that I didn't start out from nothing…. I started out with something a lot of people don't have. My dad gave me the best gift he could have when I was growing up. His time. Undivided attention and time spent with just me. Time building things together like models and RC cars. Time to teach me how to throw a curveball and to shoot a basketball. Time to take me fishing every weekend. Time to play tennis with me.

His most valuable asset. Time.

We can never have enough time. Time cannot be made. It cannot be bought. Time just fades away. Don't waste it, don't wish it by quicker. Use it fearlessly and be significant.

Citation of Resources

About Zappos Culture. (2017). Zappos Family Core Values.
    Retrieved from http://www.zappos.com/core-values

Delivering Happiness. (2014). What Is Delivering Happiness?.
    Retrieved from http://deliveringhappiness.com/company/

Wolske, Kelly & Swenk, Jason. (2016, January 6). How to Define Your Agency's
    Core Values & Setup Your Team for Success. *The Smart Agency Master
    Class*. Podcast retrieved from http://jasonswenk.com/agencys-core-values/

Entrepreneurship.org (Producer). (2011, June 12). *Core Values of Culture - Tony Hsieh
    (Zappos)*. (Video file). Retrieved from https://youtu.be/AbFIPc34AJ8

Zappos Insights. (2014, September 2). *All Hands Meeting - What It Is and Why You
    (May) Want One*. (Web log comment). Retrieved from https://www.
    zapposinsights.com/blog/item/all-hands-meeting-what-it-is-and-why-
    you-may-want-one

M. Hyatt. (2007, January 1). *Goal Setting: The 90 Day Challenge*. (Web log comment).
    Retrieved from https://michaelhyatt.com/goal-setting-the-90-day-
    challenge.html

Kruse, K. (2012, July 16). Stephen Covey: 10 Quotes That Can Change Your Life.
    Forbes. Retrieved from http://www.forbes.com/sites/
    kevinkruse/2012/07/16/the-7-habits/#6980393c2705

Albanesius, C. (2014, February 4). 10 Years Later: Facebook's Design Revolution.
    PC Mag.com. Retrieved from http://www.pcmag.com/slideshow/
    story/320360/10-years-later-facebook-s-design-evolution

The Associated Press. (2014, February 4). Timeline: Key dates in Facebook's 10-
    year history. *The Washington Times*. Retrieved from http://www.
    washingtontimes.com/news/2014/feb/4/timeline-key-dates-in-facebooks-
    10-year-history/

Buffet, W. (2003, February 21). Warren Buffett's Letters to Shareholders. Retreived from http://www.berkshirehathaway.com/letters/2002pdf.pdf

Mall, Dan & Swenk, Jason. (2016, November 16). Increasing Agency Profit with Value-Based Pricing. *The Smart Agency Master Class.* Podcast retrieved from https://jasonswenk.com/value-based-pricing/

Ross, Del & Swenk, Jason. (2014, May 6). #1 Thing Agencies Need To Do To Land the Big Clients. *The Smart Agency Master Class.* Podcast retrieved from https://jasonswenk.com/4/

Baer, J. (2012) Jay Baer Intro. (Web log comment). Retrieved from http://www.jaybaer.com/wp-content/uploads/2012/01/jay-baer-bio-for-introduction.pdf

Baer, Jay & Swenk, Jason. (2014, September 29). How to Generate Agency Business By Helping Rather Than Selling. *The Smart Agency Master Class.* Podcast retrieved from https://jasonswenk.com/generate-more-business/

Hinson, E. (2016, April 8). Why 2016 Will Be the Year of Video Marketing. (Web log comment). Retrieved from http://www.convinceandconvert.com/content-marketing/year-of-video-marketing/

Garst, Kim & Swenk, Jason. (2016, March 9). Why Your Agency Needs Live Streaming Video for Business. *The Smart Agency Master Class.* Podcast retrieved from https://jasonswenk.com/live-streaming-video-for-business/

Ehrlichman, M. (2014, April 29). 4 Tips to Go Further, Faster with Strategic Partnerships. *Entrepreneur.* Retrieved from https://www.entrepreneur.com/article/233450

Brogan, Chris & Swenk, Jason. (2015, April 28). How to Grow Your Agency By Talking to an Audience of One. *The Smart Agency Master Class.* Podcast retrieved from https://jasonswenk.com/audience-of-one/

Aileron. (2013, May 16). Stephen Covey: Why Your Small Business Needs CRM. *Forbes.* Retrieved from http://www.forbes.com/sites/aileron/2013/05/01/why-your-small-business-needs-crm/#56fc3d066e72

Dixon, M. & Adamson, B. (2011, September 30). Selling Is Not About Relationships. *Harvard Business Review.* Retrieved from https://hbr.org/2011/09/selling-is-not-about-relatio

Schaeffer, Wes & Swenk, Jason. (2015, April 28). Building the Right Sales Team to Grow Your Agency. *The Smart Agency Master Class.* Podcast retrieved from https://jasonswenk.com/building-sales-team/

DeMers, J. (2015, December 21). 5 Steps to Becoming the 'Face' of Your Company. *Entrepreneur.* Retrieved from https://www.entrepreneur.com/article/254048

Ingram, D. (2017) Behavior Modeling in the Workplace. *The Houston Chronicle.* Retrieved from http://smallbusiness.chron.com/behavior-modeling-workplace-10980.html

Economy, P. (2014, January 24). The 9 Traits that Define Leadership. *Inc.* Retrieved from http://www.inc.com/peter-economy/the-9-traits-that-define-great-leadership.html

Saylor Academy. (2012). Lesson 1.4 Ethics. *Foundations for Small Business.* Retreived from https://saylordotorg.github.io/text_small-business-management-in-the-21st-century/s05-04-ethics.html

James, G. (2013 October 7.) 10 Things Employees Want More Than a Raise. *Inc.* Retrieved from http://www.inc.com/geoffrey-james/10-things-employees-want-more-than-a-raise.html

Brose, G. (2009) Bonus Your Way to Profits. (Web log comment). Retrieved from http://www.refresher.com/agrbbonus.html

Swenk, J. (2015, October 7). Get Your Agency Bought: 3 Tips for Building a Business Worth Buying. Retrieved from https://blog.hubspot.com/agency/build-agency-buying#sm.001e9xr1r13e5fmyykz29g2el5g0o

Made in the USA
San Bernardino, CA
20 June 2018